LANGUAGE PATTERNS OF POVERTY CHILDREN

LANGUAGE PATTERNS OF POVERTY CHILDREN

By

NICHOLAS J. ANASTASIOW, Ph.D.

Indiana University
Bloomington, Indiana

and

MICHAEL L. HANES, Ph.D.

University of Florida
Gainesville, Florida

CHARLES C THOMAS · PUBLISHER
Springfield · Illinois · U.S.A.

Published and Distributed Throughout the World by

CHARLES C THOMAS • PUBLISHER

Bannerstone House

301-327 East Lawrence Avenue, Springfield, Illinois, U.S.A.

© *1976 by* CHARLES C THOMAS • PUBLISHER

ISBN 0-398-03499-0

Library of Congress Catalog Card Number 75-26854

*With THOMAS BOOKS careful attention is given to all details of
manufacturing and design. It is the Publisher's desire to present books that
are satisfactory as to their physical qualities and artistic possibilities and
appropriate for their particular use. THOMAS BOOKS will be true to those
laws of quality that assure a good name and good will.*

Library of Congress Cataloging in Publication Data

Anastasiow, Nicholas J.
    Language patterns of poverty children.

    Bibliography: p.
    Includes index.
    1. Socially handicapped children—Education—
Language arts. 2. Socially handicapped children—
Education (Primary)—United States. 3. Children—
Language. I. Hanes, Michael L., joint author.
II. Title.
LC4085.A52   371.9'67   75-26854
ISBN 0-398-03499-0

Printed in the United States of America

C-1

FOR ROBERTA AND FOR CARA AND JENA

ACKNOWLEDGEMENT

THE STUDIES REPORTED in this book owe debts to many individuals who are now scattered across the United States and Nova Scotia: Stine Levy, J. Dennis Hoban, David A. Hunter, Lewis Shapiro, James Hamilton, Sidney Mifflin, Ted Witt, Nicholas Stayrook, and Bernard Winkel. We owe debts to children in Indianapolis, Indiana; Cleveland, Tennessee; New York City, New York; Bloomington and Brown County, Indiana; Atlantic City, New Jersey. We thank Martha Dawson, founder of the Hampton Follow Through Model, for becoming associated with the schools. Dr. Mary Christian, Director of the Hampton Follow Through Model, of Hampton Institute, Virginia, has been a constant support as have the Follow Through directors and implementors of Sister Rosalie Kalley, Sister Vivian Mastromatteo, Joan Savarese, Helen Mulkene in New York City; Mamie Jackson and Ruth Thomas in Atlantic City; and Bob Erwin in Cleveland, Tennessee.

Roberta P. Anastasiow read and copy edited all early drafts and Patricia Eggleston and Madlyn A. Levine read the copy for substantive changes and made helpful suggestions. Sue Hall and Jeri Wood did much to make the final copy an accurate form.

CONTENTS

LANGUAGE PATTERNS OF
POVERTY CHILDREN

CHAPTER 1 INTRODUCTION

A PETITE FIVE-YEAR-OLD black girl sits across from an experimenter. He asks her to repeat a sentence spoken in typical school English and played on a tape recorder. The tape recorder plays the sentence: "I asked him if he did it and he said he didn't do it." She smiles, presses down the folds of her thin dress and says, "I asks him if he did it and he says he didn't did it but I knows he did." With barely a measurable delay, this five-year-old had changed or "reconstructed" the typical English spoken in the school to her own vernacular. Some persons would maintain that her English indicates that she is less intelligent, deficient in language development, or delayed in speech. We, as many others we will cite, argue that the reconstructions she made are an indication of rapid mental functioning, which indicates the child is intellectually alert. Further, we will maintain that this one anecdote can serve as an example of what masses of children, who speak a vernacular different from that of the school, do when they hear typical middle-class English: They automatically change spoken middle-class vernacular to their own. These children are capable of achieving in school. The school personnel assume that these children can understand the language of the school, which they usually can, but the school also assumes that the child will speak the language of the school which, without training, they usually cannot. Further, the school assumes that the child must begin formal reading instruction as soon as he begins first grade. We will maintain that until the child has ample experience in matching his own language with that of the school, formal reading instruction should be replaced with intensive instruction and experience in language arts. Failure to help the child master the full range of typical speech sounds of middle-class English before attempting to teach him to read begins a failure pattern all too common

3

among members of minority groups in all sections of the United States. It is both an ethnic and social-class problem. Yet interestingly, one ethnic group, the Japanese-American, has managed to shake the restrictive nature of its environment and is succeeding at comparable levels with the Anglo-Caucasian, a feat that will be discussed in detail later in the book.

This book is an attempt to present the language studies we have conducted with children from lower socioeconomic as well as minority groups over the past four years. We feel that there is a great need for teachers and administrators to reexamine their practices in the light of evidence available from a number of sources. Besides our own studies, there are many others that indicate that children who reside in poverty can succeed in school. The fact that these children are not succeeding is due more to a failure of the school to modify its practices than it is to the lacks or deficits of the child. Wilson Riles' phrase the "Child as the Victim" sums up our position. Too often we blame the child for his failure rather than plan instruction whereby the child may succeed.

HISTORIC OVERVIEW*

Historically the problem of educating masses of children of immigrant parents, the "melting pot" phenomenon, raised a few questions about genetic differences to account for the intellectual deficits of lower achievers. The achievement differences were attributed to differences in the language spoken in the home and outside of the home (bilingualism) and to the cultural shock of first-generation Americans in rejecting the patterns of the Old European-Asiatic culture and adapting to the new. These positions are ably summarized by Anastasi (1958a) in her article "Heredity, Environment and the Question 'How?'" (1958b).

The drift of the argument changed from the "cultural difference phenomenon" of the 20's to the "social-class difference" of the 40's and 50's. Allison Davis (1951) argued that achievement differences among classes were due to the bias of the tests used

---

* Portions of the following section appeared in Anastasiow (1972).

to measure intelligence and achievement. Race was not an open issue but social-class differences were. Davis had hoped to develop a culture-free test, one that did not contain bias in favor of the middle-class. It should be recalled that IQ and intelligence were synonymous terms in the earlier discussions, and the notion of a fixed IQ was widely held. Davis explained that the fact that lower-class children did poorly on aptitude measures was due to a function of the inappropriateness of the measuring instrument, particularly the Stanford-Binet. Ginsberg (1972) presents an excellent discussion of the weaknesses of existing measures of intelligence. He points out that there are four major myths concerning intelligence measures such as the Stanford Binet. The tests assume: (1) Intelligence is a unitary measure, which it is not; (2) IQ scores reflect fundamental differences in intellect rather than subcultural and motivational differences; (3) IQ tests measure competence rather than performance; and (4) IQ tests can measure innate ability unaffected by experience. What IQ tests do measure are some intellectual activities which are predominantly verbal (Ginsburg, 1972). In addition, the IQ measure assumes that all children taking the test have had an equal opportunity to master a common set of experiences and are equally motivated to do well on the test (Cronbach, 1967). Obviously, none of the above assumptions can be made for children who reside in poverty situations.

DIFFERENT OR DEFICIT

Hunt's (1961) argument changed the focus of the discussion by postulating and documenting the instability of IQ measures. In addition, he postulated that achievement differences could be due to the effects of early experience on intellectual functioning. He summarized animal and human research and postulated that the young of both species were active and curious even in situations lacking apparent rewards. Hunt stated that the long-term effect of negative environments would tend to limit children's cognitive functioning. The major body of research drawn upon to demonstrate this negative effect were the so-called maternal-separation and sensory-deprivation studies (Spitz, 1946; Bowlby, 1960; Heinicke, 1956). The positive effects of enriched environments were documented by Skodak and Skeels' (1949) study which demonstrated the superiority of the achievement of adopted children compared to those who remained in orphanages. The constructs of curiosity (Berlyne, 1965) and competence (White, 1959) were presented to account for the organism's need to transact with the environment to develop his cognitive and affective functioning. Thus, the lower-class child, particularly the inner-city child, was postulated to suffer from a deprived environment which did not allow for the active physical interaction necessary for the full development of his intellectual functioning.

LANGUAGE DIFFERENCES

What became apparent to those who worked in programs designed for the poor was that the language of these children was markedly different from that of the middle-class child. Each research position, from the drill-and-practice-oriented curriculum of Bereiter and Engelmann (1966) to the cognitive orientation of Gray and Klaus (1965), Karnes and others (1970), Weikart (1969), and Anastasiow, Stedman, and Spaulding (1970), tried to account for the language patterns of black children, which appeared to be deficits when measured by standardized tests.

Deutsch and associates (1967) proposed that the deficits were a product of a poor home environment which retarded the child's overall development. Similarly, Hess and Shipman (1965) and Deutsch (1965) perceived the deficits as products of such conditions as punitive parent-child interactions, the nonverbal communication patterns of poverty homes, and overly noisy and confusing homes.

Jensen (1969) proposed that the differences were not a product of the environment but of genetic constraints. In this position, he interpreted the *cognitive-deficit* position in terms of innate biological factors rather than as a function of environmental and child-rearing practices as Hunt had suggested and with which Hess and Shipman and Deutsch and his associates seemed to agree. Consequently, the deficit of Hunt now became two pronged: the deficit position due to environmental conditions and the deficit position due to genetic constraints.

The genetic argument has serious weaknesses. As Scarr-Salapatek (1971) has shown, genetic factors are not strong determinants of aptitude in disadvantaged groups regardless of race. However, genetic variance accounts for major differences within the socioeconomic advantaged groups. As Scarr-Salapatek states, "If all children had optimum environments for development, then genetic differences would account for most of the variance in behavior." The assumption that the poor have "optimum environments" clearly cannot be made.

LINGUISTS' VIEW

Given the verbal nature of schooling and the large proportion of verbal items on intellectual and achievement measures, it is not surprising that language, or the verbal expression of language, became the focus of the controversy. It was at this point that the linguists challenged both deficit positions and postulated that the language of poverty children was not deficient but different.

To linguists, describing any language as deficient is an untenable position. Language is acquired by all children approximately at the same time regardless of culture (Lenneberg, 1967; McNeill, 1970a). Differences appear in the surface characteristics of the language rather than in its underlying logic. Labov (1971) and Baratz and Shuy (1969) have demonstrated clearly that black inner-city children's language, while differing in surface characteristics, contains the necessary logical structures to express abstract reasoning and thought.

Labov (1972) more recently suggested that teachers expect the child to have abilities that are beyond the opportunities for language development provided children from lower socioeconomic environments. Labov's list of teacher expectations includes:

1. ability to understand spoken English (of the teacher)
2. ability to read and comprehend
3. ability to communicate (to the teacher) in spoken English
4. ability to communicate in writing
5. ability to write in Standard English grammar
6. ability to spell correctly
7. ability to use Standard English grammar in speaking

8. ability to speak with a prestige pattern of pronunciation

Labov's major point is that while the child's language is sufficient to handle his needs in his home, neighborhood and peer situations, it is different from that of the school and, consequently, the child must decode the spoken language of the teacher and make his own language match that of his teacher's.

Our observations of teachers and schooling would tend to agree with Labov: The major fallacy is the school's assumption that the child will come to school understanding the spoken English of the teacher and, further, that the teacher is *not* responsible for *teaching the child* how to understand the spoken English of the school. It has been shown that when teachers do stress spoken English and communication skills, children make significant gains in language development and score higher on Piagetian tasks (Anastasiow, 1972). These results will be presented in Chapter 7.

Further, we agree with Labov that teachers need to teach the inner-city child the rules needed to translate from the child's system to the teacher's. However, the teacher must help the child in a manner that does not belittle the child's current language. A negative evaluation of the child's language produces a negative effect on the child's self-concept.

As we will demonstrate in Chapter 4, the language of the poverty child has unique characteristics which serve his linguistic community. Any language that serves a linguistic community cannot be called a deficient language. All that can be said is that it is different from the *prestige* white, middle-class language.

SOCIAL-CLASS AND POVERTY

Social-class is not a single isolated phenomenon. It is a cluster of highly interrelated, inseparable variables. When the social-class level of the child is not taken into account, major misconceptions take place. For example, in Terman's (1925) famous gifted studies, the children who obtained high scores on the Stanford-Binet were from favorable economic conditions. One of Terman's often quoted findings is that gifted children are taller and mature more rapidly than nongifted children. This was a troublesome finding for many educators who observed that many of the gifted children in their schools were physically immature and small for their age when compared to other children. In a recent study challenging Terman's findings, Hobson (1956) was able to show that when the social-class of the child was controlled, gifted children were smaller than their age peers. Hobson concluded that Terman, in selecting bright middle-class children, confused the benefits of a favorable diet on growth and assumed that growth was an associated factor of giftedness rather than of social-class.

Social-class and economic level are positively related. The higher the social-class, the more favorable the economic conditions of the family. Hollingshead's (1965) social-class scale considers both the occupation level of the father and his number of years of formal schooling. An engineer who has a B.A. would tend to be rated lower than an engineer who possesses a Ph.D. However, Hollingshead noted that the income of an individual was not a completely accurate predictor of social-class. He also determined how many people were directly responsible to the individual. Thus, education, income, and the number of people responsible to the person became a means of estimating the relative social position of an individual.

It should be clear at this point that those members of our society at the lower end of the social-class ladder have less income, fewer years of schooling, and usually no one under their direct supervision or employment.

Poverty families are generally defined as those families who live below a certain yearly income figure. The figure varies, particularly in time of inflation, but it is usually several thousand dollars below the average yearly income.

Low income means poor diet, inadequate housing, and higher incidence of severe mental and physical disorders. To paraphrase a nursery rhyme, "when things are good, they are very, very good; when they are bad they are horrid."

In contrasting a group of mothers and children who reside in poverty to those of the middle-class, Birch and Gussow (1970) state:

The differences are profound and prolonged. Mothers of such children tend to be less well fed, less well grown, and less well cared for before they reach child-bearing age. When they reach it, they begin to bear children younger, more rapidly, and more often, and they continue to bear them to an older age. When such a mother is pregnant both her nutrition and her health will tend to be poorer than that of a woman who is better off, but she will be far less likely to get prenatal care and far more likely to be delivered under substandard conditions.

Children of such mothers are smaller at birth, die more readily, and are generally in poorer condition in infancy than are children born to the more affluent. If they survive the first month of life, their mortality thereafter is excessively high and their illnesses more frequent, more persistent, and more severe. Their early nutrition is negatively influenced by their mother's health, her age, her income level, her education, her habits and attitudes, so that among such children in the preschool years frank malnutrition, as well as subclinical manifestations of depressed nutritional status (reflected in anemia and poor growth), are markedly more prevalent. During the school years they eat irregularly, their health care continues to be almost totally inadequate, their housing is substandard, their family income is low, subsistence on public assistance is high, and family disorganization commonplace. (p. 266)

Thus, the child born into economic poverty is threatened before birth by imminent death in the period just preceding and just succeeding his birth. If he does not die, he may be maimed; if he survives with a handicap, he finds that his life is a series of lacks and that he is isolated from the mainstream of American life. Further, if he is black, Mexican-American, American Indian, Eskimo, or Oriental he may be denied basic human and civil rights in subtle and sometimes blatantly racist ways.

Robert Coles's series *Children of Crises* (1972, 1973) describes the overwhelming and deadening effect of poverty on the spirit of children who reside in its conditions. Coles speculates that the migrant child may suffer the most severe lacks. To Coles, the rootlessness of the endless car rides from camp to camp destroy the child's ability to develop beyond primitive notions of self-identity. The enslavement of migrant workers to the road boss, and their poor diet, inadequate housing, and dependence on the car for survival is a bleak picture. Many of these children drop out of life, as well as out of school, when they are six or seven. Most migrant workers die young, worn out from overwork and misuse of their bodies and spirit.

The sharecropper, although he still suffers, fares better than the migrant worker. The sharecropper has roots in the land even though the land may not belong to him.

In contrast to the migrant worker and the sharecropper, Coles feels that the Appalachian poor has a more highly developed conception of self-identity. The Appalachian's pride in his Irish-Scot heritage, as perpetuated through story and song, gives this group a sense of belonging and of family. This feeling for the land, their trust in the land, makes this group distinct.

Three novels deal with the same issues as Coles's books. Joyce Carol Oates' *A Garden of Earthly Delights* deals with the migrant worker and his identity crisis. Oates' powerful National Book Award winner *Them* portrays very effectively the Appalachian white transplanted to the city and the resulting disintegration of the family. Green's *The Doll Maker* explores a similar theme.

The movie and novel *Sounder* gives a fair portrait of the black experience and sharecropping. The moving portrait presented in *The Autobiography of Miss Jane Pitman* (both novel and television) displays the struggle and enormous effort those who reside in poverty must make to survive—not to overcome, but just to survive.

The most devastating impact of poverty on the individual is not so much in his cognitive development but in his emotional development. The migrant child's lack of self-identity deprives him of the protective security of knowing who he is and where he has come from—his family and past. Plant (1950) called this basic human security that each human must develop in order to survive *The Envelope*. He perceived The Envelope as a product of development through interactions with parents and relatives. Thus, The Envelope serves as a protective "skin" which helps the individual withstand normal daily pressures. Without it, the individual suffers from anxiety or develops patterns of behavior that lead to societal conflict.

Poverty can take its toll physically, but it also can limit the emotional development of the child. This immaturity of emotional development may in the long run be more accountable for school failure than the heretofore hypothesized cognitive deficits. How a parent views himself influences how successful a child will be in school and life. The manner in which the parent teaches the child and the parent's view of the world do much to insure the child's success or failure.

ETHNIC DIFFERENCES, SOCIALIZATION, AND SCHOOL SUCCESS

Teaching or parenting is the assisting of the child in making his own discoveries about the world. Socialization is the process whereby children are taught to see the world in the same way adults view it. What a family teaches a child are the normative beliefs held by the family and the subculture to which the family belongs.

Carlos Castaneda (1972) has described the process very well in one of his recent books in the Don Juan series. Castaneda claims that every culture teaches the child how "to see" the world in the way members of the culture perceive and define reality. To Castaneda, every member of the culture is a teacher who reinforces the child's perceptions once they become consistent with the adult accepted view of reality.

Subculture normative beliefs vary with the basic value-orientation of the total group. For example, the immigrant groups who have made the most successful transition from European and Asiatic cultures to the "melting pot" of the American culture are those who hold values similar to those of the American system. The dominant value system of the United States is the so-called Puritan ethic, which prizes, among other things, a future-goal orientation, delay of gratification, hard work, thrift, perseverance, and achievement. Both the Greek and Jewish cultures hold very similar values and have made the transition relatively easily. The Italians, Polish, and Irish, who hold somewhat different values, have had a more difficult time, with a great deal of second generation cultural conflict. Similarly, we find today that the Japanese Tokugawa ethic is very similar to the Puritan ethic, and the Japanese-American now occupy favorable economic and prestige roles in the culture. The Hawaiian, Mexican-American, Philippine (Werner, et al., 1971), and Puerto Rican (Lesser, Fifer, & Clark, 1965) cultures, which allow the child to mature slowly without environmental pressure, occupy the lowest economic positions in the United States. Thus, social classes and ethnic groups differ in terms of child-rearing practices and in their training of the child in the value orientation of what they want the child to become.

Some of these child-rearing practices and value-oriented training techniques, however, are counterproductive to the child's success in school. Let us consider for a moment what the school demands and what mothers of various social classes and ethnic groups do to prepare their children for school.

Children are capable at birth of learning about the world into which they have been born. Children of a few days old can discriminate patterns and colors. There is evidence to suggest that the child's brain at birth is a major organ of survival, and from the first day following birth the child is developing the skills which we later will call intelligence or problem solving abilities (Lipsitt, 1967, 1971).

However, although the child is marvelously equipped mentally, he still is relatively helpless physically. The child is dependent upon his caretaker, usually his mother, for food, care, and comfort. What the child does on his own is to learn about the natural phenomena of the world; for instance, that speech sounds contain meaning, that objects behind a screen are still there, that things can change shape and remain the same amount. As Piaget (1955) suggests, children learn through their experiences the basic laws of nature. What the child cannot learn by himself are the names of things and the particular language of his culture.

The American school is predominantly a verbal-oriented institution, which places primary emphasis on learning to read. The most fundamental relationship in learning to read is the degree to which the child has mastered the language orally. Parents who spend a great deal of time talking to the child and stressing the

child's use of objects and play have children who are more successful in school. (We will deal specifically with the issue in
Chapter 3.) Mothers who encourage their children in a warm
supportive environment tend to have children who mature more
rapidly. By talking to the child while diapering, feeding, and
playing, the mother provides the child samples of language.

White middle-class mothers and Sansei (third generation Japanese-American) mothers tend to use a great deal of language
while they feed, change, and bathe their babies (Caudill &
Schooler, 1973). Philippine-American, Mexican-American, Puerto
Rican-American and white lower-class mothers tend to use less
spoken language but a great deal of nonverbal communication,
such as hugs and smiles. The Philippine and Puerto Rican-American mother tends to be very indulgent about the child's acquisition of skills. There does not appear to be a press for the child to
grow rapidly.

In consequence, given the demands of the American school,
white middle-class and Sansei mothers are very skilled teachers
who provide a "hidden curriculum" in the home that prepares
their children to succeed in school. Equally bright Philippine-
American, Mexican-American, and Puerto Rican-American children do not come to school with a "set to learn," and in addition,
they have developed communication skills which are predominantly nonverbal. These children not only possess a language that
is different from that of the school but have been oriented toward
a value system that allows the child to grow at a relaxed rate.

Within all groups—white, Philippine-American, Mexican-American, Puerto Rican-American, and Japanese-American—there are
parents who are less sucessful teachers of their young children.
Unfortunately, many mothers who reside in poverty fall into
this category. These mothers tend to be authoritarian rather
than authoritative, use physical punishment to an extreme, and
are very demanding of the child's obedience. The result of such
acts is a child who is anxious, often frightened of adults, and
overly aggressive with his peers (Bandura & Walters, 1959). In
some extreme cases, the children produced by these mothers are
severely disturbed and do not possess the social skills necessary
to succeed in school (Pavanstedt, 1967).

Thus, inappropriate parenting skills may do much to interfere with normal emotional or affective development. If this is the case, the child's lack of social and self development can seriously interfere with his school success.

The question confronted by those who work with children from poverty homes is whether or not the child can be helped to succeed in school. The school's problem (not the child's) may be that the child is bilingual or speaks a different dialect, or that the child has an inadequately developed concept of self or is emotionally threatened by life and school.

In a recent summary of intervention studies with poverty children, Stedman et al. (1972) concluded that positive results can be obtained when:

1. environmental conditions of the home are modified to offset the impact of poverty in poor diet, crowded conditions, and disorganized families, thereby reducing physiological and emotional disorders;

2. parental child-rearing attitudes and techniques focus on rewarding independence and establishing achievement standards through the use of reasoning and warmth;

3. training by the parent (or intervention) begins early, before one year of age;

4. the intervention program is able to hire quality staff and to maintain a stable staff;

5. the intensity of the training program is such as to provide systematic intervention procedures based on a theoretical rationale.

The evidence to date supports the position that intelligence is a product of: (1) a healthy body with growth and maturation factors functioning; (2) direct experience in which the child experiences and then internalizes the world; (3) teaching the child the names of objects and aspects about the world; and (4) the warmth and support the parenting figure gives to the child. Parents can be very effective teachers (Schaeffer & Bayley, 1963), and parents can directly influence and modify even physiological damage which occurs before or just after birth.

In a remarkable study, *The Children of Kauai*, Werner and her colleagues (1971) followed all identified pregnancies within one year from birth to each child's tenth year. Werner was primarily interested in those conditions which lead to infant mortality and infant morbidity. More specifically, Werner wanted to identify those perinatal stress conditions which were related to later school failure.

Werner's findings are summarized as follows:

1. By age ten, differences found between children who had suffered varying degrees of perinatal complications and those who had been born without stress were less pronounced than at age two and were centered on a small group of survivors of severe perinatal stress. These survivors had a significantly higher proportion of major physical handicaps, predominantly of the central nervous, musculoskeletal, and sensory systems, as well as a higher proportion of IQs below 85 and of placements in special classes or institutions for the mentally retarded. They also had significantly lower mean-scores on the verbal comprehension, reasoning, and perceptual and numerical factors on the PMA.

2. Aside from children in institutions, no significant differences were found between children with and without perinatal complications in the proportion of poor grades obtained in basic skill subjects and in the incidence of language, perceptual, and behavioral problems.

3. Ratings of the families' socioeconomic status, educational stimulation, and emotional support showed significant associations with achievement and intellectual and emotional problems at age ten. *Ten* times more children had problems attributed to *the effects of a poor environment than to the effects of serious perinatal stress.*

4. At age ten, differences in mean PMA IQs between children growing up in the most and least favorable home environments were much larger than those between children from the most and least severely stressed groups. The effects of environmental deprivation were more powerful than was apparent at age two and accounted for much more of the variance in IQ than degree of perinatal stress.

Thus, parental teaching style is not only related to the child's success but is also related to the remediation of perinatal stress conditions. These same successful styles can be used to assist the child who resides in poverty to assume normal development. They also can be used to help the child master skills he previously has not been taught.

WHAT IS TO COME

In the next chapter we shall present a discussion of the theoretical issues and research to date dealing with language development. It is not essential for the reader unfamiliar with all the issues to read the chapter, as a discussion of stages of language development will be presented in Chapter 3. It is important to note, however, that Chapter 2 lays the groundwork for the basic assumptions concerning cognitive and language development. After reading the chapter, the reader will have a clear notion of the authors' theoretical stance. We maintain that language is acquired by the child in a social setting, and the language spoken by the child will bear all the features of the language of the family, culture, and social-class setting of the child. The child acquires language through the use of the cognitive strategies he has developed. Thus the child's language will be only as sophisticated as his cognitive development.

Secondly, we will maintain that all children develop language through a series of stages due to the fact that they develop cognitive strategies in a stage-like fashion. Children begin to acquire language from the first day of life—largely due to the fact that they begin to develop cognitive strategies from the first day of life. These latter points will be developed further in Chapter 3.

RECOMMENDED READING

Coles, R.: *Children of Crises.* Boston, Little, Brown and Co., 1967-1971, 3 vols.

Ginsburg, H.: *The Myth of the Deprived Child.* Englewood Cliffs, Prentice Hall, 1972.

Looff, D. H.: *Appalachia's Children: The Challenge of Mental Health.* The University Press of Kentucky, 1971.

CHAPTER 2 UNDERSTANDING LANGUAGE DEVELOPMENT

Development is a process that is influenced by the propensity for behavior
in an individual and the particular sequence of events that make
up his experience.

DAVID FELDMAN

IN DISCUSSING language development, psychologists frequently
disassociate the structure and content of the communicative
act from the context in which language occurs. With our over-
zealous interest in understanding the specifics of developmental
processes in the child, we tend to overlook the intent or purpose
of language. For this reason, as an introduction to this chapter,
we shall discuss the sociological significance of language in cultural units prior to our examination of the specifics of language
development.

The human species is perhaps the most distinct from other
animal species in that humans possess a creative, productive
means of transmitting cultural experiences, i.e. language. While
several psycholinguists are persistently training primates in the
use of language and observing communication in other species,
no other animal species has been observed using language in the
diverse, complex forms that man is capable of creating. While
many animal species do maintain what might be generally classi-
fied as culture or aspects of culture, man has not yet observed
other animal species transmitting from generation to generation
the content of culture through the medium of language. Culture, then, is the essence of human language, and language is a
major means by which human culture is transmitted. From this
point of view, the significance or objective of the study of child
language is to determine the course of development and sequence of acquisition by which the child becomes a competent
communicator with other members of his culture.

18

Stated in a different manner, how does the child acquire knowledge about the language to be learned; equally important, how is that knowledge expressed and comprehended in a productive manner? These questions involve four basic constructs typically mentioned in linguistic theory: competence, performance, surface structure, and deep structure.

COMPETENCE, PERFORMANCE, SURFACE STRUCTURE, DEEP STRUCTURE

The distinction between competence and performance has been traditional in linguistics (Chomsky, 1966). However, recent research has focused on psychological variables and has attempted to delineate those variables associated with deviations from hypothesized levels of competence exhibited in performance (*see* Fodor & Garrett, 1966). Performance as linguistic behavior includes the actual acts of speaking and hearing and the involvement of either encoding or decoding (McNeill, 1970b). Performance is subject to variations in individual processing rates, limitations in memory capacity, and time constraints associated with the auditory modality. In order for the individual to exercise the performance aspect of language, he must acquire knowledge of syntax, phonology, and grammatical relations—what linguists refer to as competence. In actuality, competence takes the form of a hypothetical grammar expressed by the linguist. Competence is an idealization, an abstraction, involving linguistic knowledge (Chomsky, 1965). The nature of this linguistic knowledge is hypothesized by many linguists to be in the form of transformational rules for interpreting the relationship between surface structure and deep structure.

The competence-performance distinction is similar to the distinction between surface and deep structures. Surface structure refers to the structural components of the linguistic sequence expressed in performance. Surface structure is characterized by the acoustic, phonetic, and syntactic features of utterances, such as pauses, location of articles, stress, and intonation (Chomsky & Halle, 1968; McNeill, 1970b). Deep structure is the semantic, nonlinguistic meaning or intention that is coded in a linguistic sequence of surface structures (Cazden, 1972). While specific variations in surface structures place constraints on the semantic interpretation, ultimately the underlying meaning of a linguistic sequence relies on the transformational rules available from the competence of the processor.

The notion of language universals has been derived from the organizational similarities found in the surface structures and transformational rules of diverse language (Slobin, 1971). Briefly, language universals may be defined as structural features that are common to all languages (Langacker, 1968). Obviously, universals do not refer to particular components of surface structure since the surface structures of most languages are unique in their phonological and syntactical characteristics. However, all languages do have common patterns for organizing surface structures. That is, all languages consist of phonetic components which are arranged systematically to form lexical items and syntactical structures which are used to express semantic intentions according to a particular grammar.

The distinction being made is that the universal aspects of surface structure refer to the organizational characteristics of expressed language, whereas the surface structure of a particular language refers to the unique intonation, syntactical, and phonological patterns of that language. Similarly, Chomsky (1972) distinguishes between the construction of a grammar for a particular language and a universal grammar, that is, universal characteristics of the transformational process relating speech sounds and meaning. McNeill (1970b) proposed that the universal transformations describe the essential aspects for deriving the deep structure of sentences for all languages. Examples of universal transformations include permutation, deletion, and addition. McNeill also suggested that most transformations that are unique to individual languages are idiosyncratic variations of the universal transformation types.

In essence, linguists perceive universals to be based on the common characteristics that exist among diverse languages. That is, the same general definition of the form and function of language is maintained across diverse language groups. Language everywhere consists of acoustic signals performing a universal set of communicative functions, expressing a universal set of semantic relations, and using a universal set of formal means, i.e. combining units of meaning which consist of combinations of sound units. In addition, language is grammatical, in the sense that the meaning of a message is not fully determined by any combination of the meanings of its element (Slobin, 1973).

Linguists have hypothesized that the existence of language universals is evidence to support the position that man has an innate capacity for language (Langacker, 1968; Lenneberg, 1967). McNeill concluded that language universals reflect "a specific linguistic ability and may not be a reflection of cognitive ability at all" (1970b, p. 74). The conclusion that language abilities are innate, however, does not resolve the question of how semantic notions are acquired and how cognition is subsequently expressed in language. A major theoretical issue left unresolved is how much of language acquisition is due to the characteristics of language processing and how much is due to cognition in general.

Whereas the transformational linguists have approached the issue by focusing on language, others have sought to resolve the issue by focusing on cognitions (Piaget, 1955). The relevance of hypothesizing the need of cognitive structure and organization for language acquisition may become more apparent by viewing language from a structuralist position. As presented by Piaget (1970), the structuralists consider verbal signs as only one aspect of symbolic functioning. Other forms of symbolic functioning include imitation, mental imaging, mimicking, and symbolic play (Piaget, 1951). According to the structuralist view, the development of representational thought is associated with general symbolic functioning and not just language. Therefore, the cognitive processes instrumental in the development of general symbolic functioning are also found in language acquisition.

Furthermore, Piaget maintains that language is basically a social institution, a conventional means of symbolic representation and communication. Conventional symbols have developed within languages for representing and identifying meaning even though the relationship between sound and meaning is indirect and arbitrary. For example, the relationship between sound and meaning becomes quite distinct in adult speech perception. Pisoni (1971) demonstrated that phoneme categories are consistently imposed on a continuum of acoustic signals which gradually progress from one distinct phoneme to a contrasting phoneme. Therefore, the conventional symbols used in language are not arbitrary in the same sense as individual symbols used in symbolic games and dreams (Piaget, 1970). The idiosyncratic symbols in dreams and symbolic games are functional only in the symbol-meaning relationship created by the individual (Piaget, 1951).

According to Piaget (1970), the development of representational thought is dependent on the processes of cognitive maturation. Therefore, whether the processes involve an idiosyncratic or a conventional symbolic system, the complexity of the relationship between the symbol and meaning is dependent on the level of cognitive development attained by the child. Piaget perceives the development of cognitive processes as proceeding through a series of invariant stages from sensorimotor to preoperational, concrete operations, and formal operations. Piaget proposes that sensorimotor thought is basically motor patterns based on physical actions. These action schemas form the basis for preoperational thought and the development of symbolic functioning. Piaget (1955) concluded that during the sensorimotor and early concrete-operational stages the child directly associates words or images (signifiers) with the referant perceptual object or event (significate). Symbolic functioning begins with the differentiation of signifiers from significates. Even after the child is able to differentiate signifiers from significates in representational thought, he continues to use earlier acquired sensorimotor forms of thought processing. Sensorimotor thought processes are characterized by the recall of analogy patterns of processing which are idiosyncratic to the individual. Therefore, the early representational thought-patterns do not contain the logical patterns of organization and structure that are inherent with social symbol systems. In this respect, the acquisition of language, or other similar socialized systems of representation, makes thought conscious (Piaget, 1928). That is, language provides conventional symbols for representation as well as a systematic means for relating symbols in processing or expressing semantic intentions (Sinclair-de Zwart, 1969). Therefore, with the development of symbolic functioning, language becomes a useful means of coding semantic intentions for storage and retrieval processes in memory (Inhelder, et al., 1966).

The basic processes in the development of cognitive structures are considered to be conceptualization and categorization, which involve the extraction of differences and similarities (Flavell, 1963). Vygotsky (1962) concluded that cognitive development proceeds from processing the whole to the particular, that is, in Piagetian terms, from syncretism to analysis. According to Piaget (1962), syncretistic perceptions are wide and comprehensive but also obscure and undifferentiated. Analytic perceptions, however, include perceptions of the separate units as well as the systematic relationships between separate units comprising the whole perception. The basis for the development of analytic processes is the progressive differentiation of signifiers (the symbol) and significates (the concept being represented). Since adults have differentiated between signifiers and significates, Lenneberg (1967) proposed that the abstract relationship between words and meaning is mediated by the process of conceptualization. In Lenneberg's view, words serve as surface markers or references for the conceptualization process by which meaning is derived.

Slobin (1973) emphasizes the relationship of the complexity of linguistic rule systems and development of cognitive processes for acquiring linguistic transformational rules. In a review of cross-cultural language acquisition studies, he proposed a set of cognitive prerequisites which apply to the acquisition of all languages. Slobin maintained that the child must be able to recognize the relationship between physical or social events and their expression in an acoustic event in order to construct rules for processing language. Also, according to Slobin, the child must be able to process, organize, and store linguistic information. These cognitive prerequisites are related to the two basic components of a social symbolic system discussed earlier; that is, symbols and systematic rules for relating symbols. Significant, however, is the fact that, according to Piagetian theory, the cognitive prerequisites proposed by Slobin develop gradually and are subject to the general characteristics and limitations of cognitive developmental stages. For instance, according to Piaget (1951), symbolic functioning evolves from sensorimotor thought. The sensorimotor schemas persist in early representational thought to the extent that social symbols acquired during the transition period between sensorimotor and preoperational stages are considered by the child as individual symbols (Flavell, 1963). However, the cognitive structures used in symbolic functioning are constantly changing as the child assimilates information from the social environment and accommodates acquired structures. The gradual progression of this assimilation-accommodation process eventually leads to a temporary state of equilibrium between social-environment information and acquired cognitive structures. Various investigators have suggested that these states of equilibrium may be described by a set of principles that the child develops for processing language (Bever, 1970; Slobin, 1973).

To summarize, the linguistic constructs of competence, performance, deep structure, and surface structure have been discussed. In exploring the interrelationships among these constructs, this writer suggests that the linguistic structure (i.e. phonetic and syntactic components known as surface structure) of utterances or expressions (performance) is transformed by the knowledge of systematic rules (competence) into an underlying semantic intention (deep structure). Consequently, it is proposed that the major problem for developmental psycholinguistics is to account for the acquisition of social symbols (words) which operate as signifiers for an underlying semantic intention, as well as the acquisition of knowledge about the systematic relationships utilized in generating linguistic sequences.

The development of representational thought was discussed in relation to the acquisition of symbolic systems in the child. The essence of representational thought was considered to be the basic processes of conceptualization and categorization which are evidenced by increased differentiation over the course of development. The basic structures of order, deletion, and substitution found in early cognitive development (Piaget, 1970) are similar to the universal transformation types suggested by linguistic theory. The conclusion may be drawn that the linguistic construct of deep structure is fundamentally equivalent to the construct of cognitive structure derived from developmental psychology. Accepting this conclusion, however, does not answer the question as to how the child acquires a specific social symbol-system, i.e. a native language. In an attempt to clarify the process of acquiring a specific language, Brown (1973) proposed that the complexity of the symbols and of the organizational rules for expression (linguistic complexity) interact with the degree to which cognitive structures for processing symbolic representations have developed (cognitive complexity).

LANGUAGE AND THOUGHT

Accepting Brown's proposition leads to two basic questions about the acquisition of language. First, if linguistic complexity and cognitive complexity interact in the process of language acquisition, how is this interaction manifested and subsequently identified over the course of development? Secondly, if the developmental stages of cognition are universal, is the acquisition of semantic notions and linguistic forms expressing these notions universal within a language family as well as across dialectal groups?

Ultimately, answers to the above questions involve the development of semantic structures and an explanation of the relative complexity of various linguistic forms. However, a prior question involves the relationship between language acquisition and cognitive development in the developing child.

Lenneberg (1967) concluded that not only can cognition develop in the absence of knowledge of any language, but also the development of language appears to require a certain minimum state of maturity and specificity of cognition. Similarly, Piaget (1970) stated that cognition precedes language ontogenetically and that language develops out of the maturation of cognitive processes. An extension of this position would suggest that early language development has a minimal effect on cognitive development but is dependent upon a minimal level of cognitive development.

The most convincing evidence concerning the primacy of cognitive development comes from the research on the cognitive development of deaf children. Although deaf children generally acquire a form of symbolic communication much later than normal children, Furth (1964) concluded that the lack of language does not affect cognitive development in any direct or decisive manner. In addition, the evidence from research with mental retardates suggests that cognitive development is an essential factor in language development (Anastasiow & Stayrook, 1972; Semmel, 1966). Similarly, attempts to increase the rate of cognitive development in normal children by teaching the vocabulary needed in order to function at a higher level of cognition have been generally unsuccessful (e.g. Sinclair-de Zwart, 1969).

Summarizing similar evidence in support of the primacy of cognitive development hypotheses, Slobin (1971) concluded that particular linguistic forms are not comprehended nor produced until the underlying cognitive aspects are developed. The order of acquisition of locatives, for example, seems to follow the sequence of cognitive developmental stages (Slobin, 1973). Other evidence may be interpreted in support of a similar relationship between level of cognitive development and the syntactical or surface structure characteristics of child language. For instance, Piaget (1970) proposed that prior to symbolic functioning, the cognitive operations of order, subordination, and correspondence have developed in sensorimotor intelligence. Similarly, retention of original word order is a very common characteristic of young children's sentence imitations (Brown & Fraser, 1963; Fraser, Brown & Bellugi, 1963; Slobin & Welsh, 1973). In addition, Menyuk (1969) found increasing use of the syntactic operations of addition, deletion, substitution, and permutation in the speech produced by four- to seven-year-old children. Although chronological age is not an exact indicator of cognitive development, the age range of four to seven years consistently appears in research studies as the transition period between preoperational and concrete operations. This transition period is characterized by the development of reversible schemas (Flavell, 1963) which form the basis of the syntactical operations observed by Menyuk.

Maintaining a position that the processes of development are integrated, a series of relationships can be proposed among the development of cognitive structures, language development, and the acquisition of meaning or semantic structures. Cognitive structures may be viewed as the mediating processes that interpret the relationship between physical events or symbolic representations and their meaning in semantic structures. Hence, both the content and expression of semantic structures are dependent on the development of cognitive structures. The evidence presented above supports the Piagetian view that cognitive functioning exists during the sensorimotor stage and prior to the acquisition of a social system of symbolic representation. However, the characteristics of sensorimotor cognitive structures determine the form and content of the semantic structures.

Due to the nature of the cognitive structures that function in early symbolic functioning, some theorists take as supportive evidence the finding that the first words acquired by the child refer to objects and actions in the environment (Brown, 1973). It appears that the child processes and uses social symbols acquired during early symbolic functioning as part of his idiosyncratic symbol system (Flavell, 1963). Additional evidence from word-sorting tasks (Miller, 1969), free-recall tasks, and recall of hierarchically structured material (Bower, et al., 1969) has demonstrated that young children, as compared to adults, exhibit a more idiosyncratic and concrete lexical organization.

All formal symbol systems consist of representational symbols as well as rules for relating symbols. Therefore, it is to be expected that as cognitive structures differentiate symbols into classes, the earliest classes to develop will be related to basic relationships within the system. In this respect, McNeill (1966b) has shown that young children categorize linguistic symbols primarily according to grammatical class features, i.e. noun, verb.

Further support is found in Anderson and Beh (1968) who

demonstrated a shift from grammatical classification processes to more abstract semantic classification during the transitional period between preoperational and concrete operations stages. McNeill (1970a) described this shift in semantic classification as a shift from syntagmatic (grammatical class) to paradigmatic (conceptual class) processing. McNeill hypothesized that the shift occurs as a function of the horizontal differentiation of semantic structures (i.e. differentiation within a class of semantic features). Vertical semantic differentiation involves the acquisition of new classes of semantic features and apparently occurs simultaneously with horizontal development (McNeill, 1970b). The lack of horizontal differentiation is evidenced in sentence completion and story-telling tasks with young children. In these tasks, young children frequently invert cause-effect relations and are unable to differentiate causality of sequence and causality of justification (Piaget, 1928; Vygotsky, 1962). Piaget observed that young children use connective forms like *because* and *but* only in a general sense as a coordinate connective. It appears that the child in preoperational and concrete operations stages is unable to differentiate the semantic implications conveyed in various members of the connective class.

Therefore, the developmental trend in semantic development is characterized by an increase in class complexity as well as an increase in the number of classes. Perfetti (1972) summarized several studies by concluding that the process of semantic-feature acquisition appears to be ordered so that later-acquired features are increasingly abstract. Further, Slobin (1971) pointed out that from the time the child puts two words together, child language is structured and characterized by hierarchical structures, regularity, and changes with age.

Characteristics similar to those found in semantic development also describe the development of cognitive structures in Piagetian theory. Furth summarized the Piagetian view by stating that "the active, transformational aspect of thinking within the context of a structure, increasing in scope and internal complexity, is the unifying link between the earliest manifestation of intelligent thinking (preoperational action-schemas) and mature logical thinking (formal operations)" (1967, p. 820).

Subsumed in the Piagetian position is the relational context in which structures develop. That is, cognitive structures do not develop in isolation, one from another; relationships develop between structures giving a systematic network of cognitive structures. The nature of these relationships between cognitive structures will depend on the functional characteristics of the cognitive structures and the characteristics of the stage of development attained by the child. This conception of interrelated structures in semantic development is quite similar to that proposed by Riegel (1970). Riegel hypothesized that the development of semantic features involves the acquisition of feature classes and feature-class differentiation as well as the development of referential relationships between classes.

As a brief review, an initial proposition in this section is that cognitive development precedes language development. In relation to language acquisition, Slobin summarized this position in stating that "new forms express old functions, and new functions are first expressed by old forms (1973, p. 184; *see also* Werner & Kaplan, 1963). This writer proposes that if distinctions between cognitive structures and semantic structures were made, then clearer descriptions of the interaction between cognitive and language development could be defined.

In the position presented, the functional purpose of cognitive structures is the interpretation of perceptual events into semantic structures, whereas the functional purpose of language is the communication of semantic intentions. In the specific case of language processing, cognitive structures function as interpretive processes in the derivation of semantic content from expressions as well as in the formulation of expressions from semantic intentions. Given these basic relationships, a series of propositions may be stated as follows:

1. Cognitive structures are functionally similar to the linguistic construct of competence.
2. Semantic structures in this position can be equated with the linguistic construct of deep structure.
3. The interpretation of semantic intentions into language expressions is dependent upon the development of cognitive structures.

4. The comprehension of linguistic expressions is dependent on the accessible means in cognitive structures for interpreting symbolic representations.
5. There is a direct relationship between the linguistic complexity of expression and the cognitive complexity required for interpreting the semantic intentions of the expression.
6. The rate of acquisition for expressive forms varies according to the complexity of the linguistic forms and the complexity of cognitive structures required for derivation of the semantic intentions.

RECOMMENDED READING

Slobin, D. I.: *Psycholinguistics.* Glenview, Scott, Foresman, 1971.

CHAPTER 3 STAGES OF LANGUAGE ACQUISITION

To understand stages of development is still the
"great mystery."

J. PIAGET

CHILDREN'S LANGUAGE has always interested most adults, whether they have studied children's speech extensively or were
amazed by the intriguing and often humorous speech children
produce. Those who have studied aspects of child language find
it especially intriguing in that specific analysis of children's
speech reveals systematic and logical stages in the acquisition
process. Perhaps "systematic stages" best describes the acquisition
process since children's logic is often confusing to the adult
mind. This chapter focuses on specific aspects in the acquisition
of linguistic or language structures. The latter portion discusses
the development of a meaning or semantic system for processing
of intentions encoded in linguistic communications. In simpler
terms, our discussion focuses on how the child becomes a competent user of language.

In the process of language acquisition, the child is essentially
acquiring two categories of knowledge about language: (1)
knowledge of symbols for representation, i.e. knowledge of
words, and (2) knowledge of organizational rules for expressing
notions in a symbolic form, i.e. knowledge of acceptable sentence structure. First, the relationship between symbol and meaning is arbitrary and dependent on the language being spoken,
that is, dependent in the sense that a social group has agreed at
some time to represent an event with a particular symbol. For example, the word *boat* in English refers to a type of vessel usually used for transportation in water, while the word *bateau* in
French refers to the same object. Secondly, the rules for organiz-

ing symbols in an expression are arbitrary and applicable only in respect to a particular language. The commonly used noun-subject/verb-predicate organization in English is linguistically comparable to the noun-subject/verb-predicate construction in Russian and the noun-predicate-verb in German. Consequently, the child (or adult) learning a language is faced with the problems of learning conventional symbols as well as the conventional means of organizing those symbols in a given language group. While it may be argued that each language is logically structured, the logic of any language is dependent on the rules of organization accepted by the given society and not necessarily explainable by a formal means of logic. The following sections will discuss specific aspects of language development in respect to phonology, syntax, and semantics.

PHONOLOGICAL DEVELOPMENT

From the parent's view, one of the most exciting milestones in their child's early life is the utterance of the first distinguishable word. In all probability, the first word to appear in a baby's vocabulary will be "mama" or "papa." While most parents will smile with pride and proclaim that their child has recognized the primary caretakers by naming them, the linguist will point out that p and m are among the first consonants to appear in children's speech and are accompanied by a vowel such as a (McNeill, 1970b). As can be seen, the developmental linguist studying phonological development is concerned with aspects of language acquisition much more specific than pronunciation of words. The study of phonology encompasses linguistics, physics, physiology, and anatomy. Our discussion will be limited to the questions related to the acquisition and discrimination of sound classes or phonemes.

Frequently phonological development is discussed in terms of the acquisition and comprehension of differences in phonemes or distinctive features (Jacobson, 1968). Distinctive features refer to the physical and physiological attributes which are essential in order to produce a particular sound. For example, McNeill described the consonant p as follows:

P is a consonant formed at the front of the mouth; it is a stop; it is unvoiced; it represents a nearly total absence of acoustic energy. (1970, p. 133)

The various combinations of a small number of distinctive features can describe the complete range of sounds in the English language.

Various researchers have concluded that the acquisition of sound classes or phonemes may be hierarchically arranged in relation to distinctive features (Menyuk, 1968a; Jacobson, 1968; Olmsted, 1968). The basic notion to hierarchically arranging phonemes by distinctive features is that easily discriminated sound classes are acquired first, while classes that are more difficult to discriminate are acquired later. Even though a limited amount of evidence is available, the analyses of children's spontaneous speech samples indicate that phonemes do appear to follow the sequence that is predicted from the hierarchical arrangement of phonemes in order of discriminability.

Given in Table I are the results of three studies indicating at what age children correctly produce particular consonant sounds. The reader should note that even with the criteria of correct production 75 percent of the time, some of the consonants are not mastered until the age of seven years.

Equally important to mention is the fact that children who speak a dialect may not clearly pronounce consonants in the final position of a word. This aspect of dialect will be discussed in more detail in Chapter 5. The person working with dialect speakers does need to recognize, even at the phonological level, the difference between errors in production due to development and changes that children make that are consistent with a dialect.

A major problem in phonological development involves our incomplete knowledge of the development of auditory perceptual ability in young children. There is only a small amount of data on the development of children's speech discrimination ability, since spontaneous speech sampling and similar measures of production have been major techniques in child language study. Based on the available data on receptive speech, it does ap-

TABLE I

COMPARISON OF THE AGES AT WHICH SUBJECTS CORRECTLY
PRODUCED SPECIFIC CONSTANT SOUNDS IN THE TEMPLIN,
THE WELLMAN, AND THE POOLE STUDIES*

Phonetic Symbol	Orthographic Symbol	Key Word	Age Correctly Produced Templin (1957)	Wellman (1931)	Poole (1934)
/m/ .... m		monkey	3	3	3.5
/n/ .... n		nickel	3	3	4.5
/ŋ/ .... ng		ring	3	—ᵃ	4.5
/p/ .... p		potatoe	3	4	3.5
/f/ .... f		fork	3	3	5.5
/h/ .... h		hat	3	3	3.5
/w/ .... w		water	3	3	3.5
/j/ .... y		yellow	3.5	4	4.5
/k/ .... k		kitten	4	4	4.5
/b/ .... b		baby	4	3	3.5
/d/ .... d		dog	4	5	4.5
/g/ .... g		gun	4	4	4.5
/r/ .... r		radio	4	5	7.5
/s/ .... s		see	4.5	5	7.5ᵇ
/ʃ/ .... sh		shoe	4.5	—ᶜ	6.5
/tʃ/ .... ch		church	4.5	5	—ᶜ
/t/ .... t		tiger	6	6	4.5
/θ/ .... th		thin	6	—ᵃ	7.5ᵇ
/v/ v		vase	6	5	6.5ᵇ
/l/ l		lamp	6	4	6.5
/ð/ .... th		then	7	—ᶜ	6.5
/z/ .... z		zipper	7	5	7.5ᵇ
/ʒ/ .... zh		measure	7	—ᶜ	6.5
/dʒ/ .... j		jar	7	6	—ᶜ
/hw/ .... wh		whistle	—ᵃ	—ᵃ	7.5

* In the Wellman and others, and Templin studies a sound was considered mastered if it was articulated correctly by 75 percent of the subjects. The criterion of correct production was 100 percent in the Poole study.

ᵃ Sound was tested but was not produced correctly by 75 percent of the subjects at the oldest age tested. In the Wellman data the "hw" reached the percentage criterion at 5 but not at 6 years, the medial "n" reached it at 3, and the initial and medial "θ" and "ð" at 5 years.

ᵇ Poole (Davis, 1938), in a study of 20,000 preschool and school-age children reports the following shifts: "s" and "z" appear at 5.5 years, then disappear and return later at 7.5 years or above; "θ" appears at 6.5 years and "v" at 5.5 years.

ᶜ Sound not tested or not reported.

Adapted from: Templin, M. C. Certain language skills in children, their development and interrelationships. Institute of Child Welfare, Monograph Series, No. 26, 54. Minneapolis: University of Minnesota Press, 1957.

pear that very young infants do perceive and respond to changes in linguistic stimulation (Condon & Sander, 1974a, b; Eimas et al., 1971). While the contention that the basic sound-meaning relationship may be established quite early in the life of a child, a great deal of careful study needs to be done before clear-cut conclusions about the development of linguistic perceptual abilities can be made. It is known, however, that infants will listen to speech sounds very early in life, and if given a preference, will listen to speech rather than music or other sounds (Butterfield & Cairns, 1974). This has led Eimas to suggest that a speech detection ability may be an innate characteristic of man. What also is known is that the changes in a child's utterances are due in part to the child's increasing ability to control his vocal apparatus. Some sounds are impossible for a baby to make until his head is in a position more directly over his throat—a developmental achievement at about six months.

Our knowledge of phonological development during early childhood, and especially during the early school years, is still not complete.

A survey of the research literature suggests that there are two major factors affecting phonological development during the early childhood years. As in any area of development requiring muscular coordination, one factor is the physical maturation of the child. Even adults are subject to errors in attempting to correctly pronounce words involving particular phonemic clusters. While adults' mispronunciation may be due to factors other than simple physical coordination, the point remains that several speech sounds require complex coordination of the articulators in the vocal tract. Many children around the age of five years have problems clearly pronouncing the /l/sound (Palermo & Molfese, 1972). Part of the problem appears to be related to the manipulation of the tongue in the process of producing the sound.

Young children have difficulty not only pronouncing some sounds separately but also producing sounds in the medial position of a word. Sounds in the initial position of a word appear to cause few errors in pronunciation, while sounds in final position are slightly more difficult to pronounce. Apparently sounds in the medial position of a word are the most difficult to pronounce even throughout adulthood (MacNeilage, 1970). The data summarized in Table II demonstrate this conclusion. Notice the small amount of change across age groups in the percentage of subjects misarticulating particular consonants.

TABLE II

THE TEN MOST FREQUENTLY MISARTICULATED CONSONANTS
AS REPORTED IN SEVERAL STUDIES*

Hall (children) (1939)		Hall (adults) (1939)		Roe & Milisen (Grade I) (1942)		Roe & Milisen (Grade VI) (1942)	
Sound	% of S's	Sound	% of S's	Sound	% of S's	Sound	% of S's
s	90.5	s	83.1	dʒ	91.2	z	84.5
z	47.6	z	75.9	z	88.1	dʒ	70.7
ʃ	47.6	dʒ	48.2	d	70.1	d	68.8
tʃ	42.9	ʃ	37.3	g	69.1	t	55.6
dʒ	33.3	tʃ	34.9	θ	68.8	hw	44.7
ʒ	28.6	hw	28.9	ð	57.3	θ	45.1
hw	23.8	ʒ	10.8	v	53.0	ð	41.4
θ	23.8	ð	10.8	s	48.9	g	39.7
r	19.0	ŋ	9.6	t	45.7	v	38.4
ð	9.5	θ	7.2	b	26.0	s	32.8

Roe & Milisen (Grades I-VI) (1942)		Roe & Milisen (all grades and) excluding voiced or voiceless errors) (1942)		Sayler (all grades) (1949)		Sayler (all grades and excluding voiced or voiceless errors) (1949)	
Sound	% of Error	Sound	% of Error	Sound	% of Error	Sound	% of Error
z	45.8	θ	30.3	hw	29.6	z	17.4
hw	40.0	s	19.7	z	28.9	v	9.3
θ	30.3	t	14.0	ð	19.6	tʃ	9.3
dʒ	30.2	ð	13.2	v	12.6	n	9.2
d	25.0	z	12.4	tʃ	9.3	ð	9.0
s	19.9	dʒ	7.2	ŋ	9.2	hw	7.1
g	18.5	tʃ	6.4	f	3.1	f	3.1
ð	16.5	r	5.9	g	2.8	s	2.7
v	16.0	v	5.6	s	2.7	θ	2.6
t	14.0	k	4.7	θ	2.6	g	2.4

* The percentage of subjects making errors or the percentage of errors on each sound is given. The sound was considered in error if it was misarticulated in any word position tested.

Source: Templin, M. C. Certain language skills in children, their development and interrelationships. *Institute of Child Welfare, Monograph Series*, No. 26, 54. Minneapolis: University of Minnesota Press, 1957.

The child learning a language must learn the rules which govern the pronunciation of sound clusters or the combination of sounds as well as the articulation of separate sounds. For this reason, it is understandable that even children in middle childhood have problems with consonant blends that involve a rapid series of complicated articulatory gestures unrelieved by interruption of an easier vowel sound. Similarly the errors that do occur in production appear to be substitutions with subtle distinctive differences. For example, plosives are substituted by other plosives, fricatives are replaced by other fricatives.

Another factor in speech development is lateralization of speech on the left side of the brain. Although this process of lateralization begins as early as one week of age, it is not complete until the child is four or five years of age. There are some indications that lateralization may be completed even later for lower-class children, a factor which may be involved in lower-class children's difficulties in school-related tasks (Schiefelbusch & Lloyd, 1973).

Undoubtedly the development of a phonological system is the basis upon which the child acquires a language. Yet our knowledge of the fundamental processes involved is limited. We do know that clear pronunciation of speech sounds is partially a function of physical maturation. The extent to which perceptual or discriminatory abilities limit or enhance the acquisition of speech sounds is at this point in time unknown.

SYNTACTIC DEVELOPMENT

From the time the child begins putting two words together, child language is systematically structured and constantly changing (Slobin, 1971). The manner in which the child systematically structures his language and the changes in that structure have provided the topic for a great deal of language development research in recent years. Our knowledge of syntactic development, unlike that of phonological development, is much greater and more diverse in theoretical orientations.

Perhaps the greatest influence on the study of child language structure has been the development of transformational grammar. Transformational grammar may be defined as a set of hypothetical rules for translating sentences into their underlying meaning. Interest in the development of transformational rules has stimulated studies of the structure of children's language. As a result of these studies, some researchers contend that by the age of five years children have acquired all of the basic transformational rules present in the adult system (e.g., Menyuk, 1968b). While the basic transformational rules are obviously operations which do not require a fully developed language system, equally obvious to those who have worked with young children is the fact that much language is acquired after the age of five (Palermo & Molfese, 1972). Perhaps the most evident conclusion from the child language research is that the structure of children's language is not a simplified version of adult language. The unique structure of child language and the progressive changes in that structure provide the focus in our discussion of syntactic development.

Even prior to the time children begin putting words together or in combination, many parents will tell you that their child is capable of expressing his intentions in one-word sentences. Many times these one-word sentences involve words that the child has created and that are understood only by the parents or siblings. For example, "wa-wa" may mean "I want some milk" or "Where is my cup?" As simple as these examples may seem, any parent can provide similar examples from experience with their child. This type of one-word sentence is generally referred to as holophrasic speech, meaning that children may express complex ideas in one word. McNeill (1970a, b) suggested that there are three main characteristics of holophrasic speech: connotative, expressive, and referential. The significant point, however, is that in order for the adult to be able to translate holophrasic speech into full linguistic expressions, a knowledge of the contextual cues as well as a knowledge of the child's symbol system is required. Without this knowledge, the adult must resort to a trial and error method of attempting to translate the child's intentions. Similarly, the child is faced with the tasks of acquiring a conventional symbol system and a conventional means of expressing the contextual information in order to become a competent communicator with language.

In the early 1960's three major studies were initiated as separate attempts to describe the grammar of child language. A partial result of these studies was the development of a type of grammar for early speech patterns. Distributional analyses of spontaneous speech samples indicated that two basic classes of words occur in early speech patterns. Braine (1963) called these two classes of words the pivot class and the open class. The pivot class typically includes a small number of words which are used frequently. The open class includes many more words which are used less frequently. While words from the open class may appear alone or together, words from the pivot class may never appear alone or with each other. McNeill (1970b) has summarized the pivot and open classes of three children studied by Bellugi and Brown (1964), Braine (1963), and Miller and Ervin (1964). Notice the number of possible combinations that are available to the child, as well as the variety of meanings that can be communicated.

Once the child has begun producing multi-word sentences, the pivot-open classification becomes less useful for describing child language. Brown and Fraser (1963) described the early multi-word sentences of very young children as telegraphic. Telegraphic aptly describes a basic characteristic of many children's early sentences in that the sentences are similar to adult sentences in structure yet frequently lack function words much like a telegram. Function words or functors refer to articles, connectives, auxillary verbs, copular verbs, and inflections, such as "The," "and," "have," "be," and "ing." Some commonly observed examples are "Where Mommy go?" and "Put sock on."

Brown (1973) contends that functors are not present in early speech patterns because they are difficult to acquire. He analyzed the acquisition of various functor forms and concluded that the grammatical complexity and the abstractness of a word such as "the" are major factors limiting the number of functor forms found in early speech samples.

Most adults are aware of the generalization that as a child becomes a more competent user of language his language becomes increasingly complex. A more difficult problem to solve is to determine in what ways a child's language system becomes more

TABLE III

PIVOT AND OPEN CLASSES FROM THREE STUDIES OF
CHILD LANGUAGE

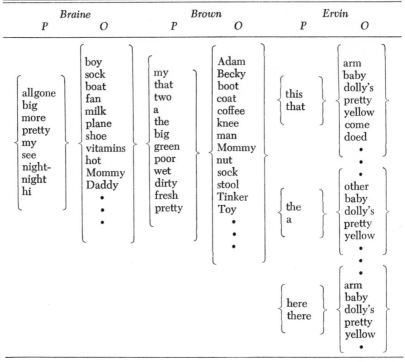

Braine		Brown		Ervin	
P	O	P	O	P	O
allgone big more pretty my see night- night hi	boy sock boat fan milk plane shoe vitamins hot Mommy Daddy · · ·	my that two a the big green poor wet dirty fresh pretty	Adam Becky boot coat coffee knee man Mommy nut sock stool Tinker Toy · · ·	this that the a here there	arm baby dolly's pretty yellow come doed · · · other baby dolly's pretty yellow · · · arm baby dolly's pretty yellow ·

Source: McNeill, D.: Developmental psycholinguistics. In F. Smith and G. A. Miller (Eds.): The Genesis of Language: A Psycholinguistic Approach. Cambridge, M.I.T. Press, 1966.

complex. We have discussed early speech patterns and the increasing complexity in terms of the length of sentences and the increased use of word classes which approximate adult sentence structure. Somewhat less obvious changes occur in relation to the use of more diverse and appropriate verb forms to relate time of action in relation to other events.

The acquisition of verb forms provides an excellent example of a phenomenon found in various aspects of syntactic development. The fact that young children frequently produce sentences such as "He comed home" and "She runned to the store" is rather common knowledge to parents and teachers. The verb forms in these sentences illustrate the phenomenon of regularization or overgeneralization. That is, children tend to regularize verb forms which have irregular forms in adult speech, i.e. "goed." While we might conclude that this is a simple process by which the child is learning the appropriate endings for verbs and nouns, the actual development of irregular forms is much more complex. Although we may become aware of the child's attempt to express intentions related to time because of the occurrence of overgeneralization, children initially express irregular forms correctly prior to overgeneralization (Ervin, 1964). Once the child begins expressing regular past tense verbs correctly, all verbs are regularized and may remain so for an extended period of time. Apparently a major factor in the reduction of overgeneralization is experience with the language, since frequent exposure to irregular forms in adult language is considered as an explanation for their correct usage prior to regularization.

The fact that overgeneralization does occur makes it difficult to conclude that children are acquiring specific forms alone. If this were the case, children would infrequently overgeneralize previously correct irregular forms. The logical conclusion is that children are attempting to develop a rule system by which to govern the production of linguistic expressions in a variety of situations. In addition, if child language was merely a simplified version of the adult language structure, then we would expect to find a match between adult and child language structure.

SEMANTICS ON THE DEVELOPMENT OF MEANING

Very early in a child's life it appears that children try to figure out how the world operates. Children can be observed scanning their mothers' faces, watching lights and rolling objects, or studying in complete absorption the movements of a mobile (Lipsitt, 1967). When speech first appears, it now seems clear that the child's first words are attempts to name things he already knows about—for example "ball," "car," "cookie," or "doggie." Katherine Nelson (1974) found that a child who had many toys to play with tended to name toys rather than persons. Nelson also observed that children would make up names for things if an adult was not around to supply the right name or if the adult failed to understand the child's intent.

A major point to be made is that the first words the child speaks are words that refer to objects or persons or actions he already understands. The implication here is that the development of a meaning system is closely related to the characteristics of developing cognitive processes.

Palermo and Molfese (1972) recently reviewed the literature on language development in children after the age of five. A major conclusion from their review was that significant changes in language and the semantic systems are correlated with transitional periods in cognitive development. In other words, as the child is able to cognitively process increasingly complex information, his language system will become increasingly complex. McNeill (1970) has described two basic processes in the development of a meaning system, horizontal and vertical structuring. Horizontal structuring refers to the process by which symbols or words enter the meaning system with an incomplete set of semantic features for establishing the use and meaning of that symbol. An example would be a child increasing the definitions of a word like "dog" to mean his own pet and then all other dogs. Vertical structuring refers to the process by which words are understood with a complete set of meanings; future development, involving the addition of new words. The result is that a child possesses knowledge of words much like a dictionary. The research literature suggests that cognitive processes are instrumental in the development of a fully functioning meaning system (Palermo & Molfese, 1972).

Chapter 4 will explore more fully the relationship between cognition and semantic development in the young child. Table IV, however, illustrates the systematic progression of increasing complexity in all aspects of language development.

As can be seen in Table IV, phonological, syntactic, and semantic development is interrelated and interdependent. Consequently, the study of each of these aspects of language development is included in the question posed at the beginning of this chapter; that is, how does the child become a competent

TABLE IV

DEVELOPMENT ACHIEVEMENTS

Age	Activity
0-3 months	activity dominated by reflexes response motorically to speech attends to sounds, identifies mother's voice tracks visually moving objects differentiated crying related to varying needs
3-6 months	babbles, produces wide range of phonetically related sounds imitates previously acquired sounds when presented by another person looks at and studies objects
6-12 months	babbling and jargon, matches intonation patterns active manipulation and grasping crawling, attempts at walking identifies familiar objects
12-18 months	jargon and inflection intonation one word sentences and naming objects, actions walking active manipulation and coordination of complex movements
18-24 months	two words sentences ("My ball," "Ball gone") walking, climbing object constancy/permanence
2-5 years	complete sentences in simple forms relates to observable action, thought dominated by perception
5-7 years	acquires passive construction begins to overcome perceptual dominance relates to observable actions

user of language? In their search for the answer to this question, linguists and developmental psycholinguists have derived features which are common to all languages and the acquisition of language.

A recent statement by John Joyner of the American Speech and Hearing Association says it well.

Modern linguists are involved in the study of human speech and language, including the nature, structure, and modification of language. They have searched for universal foundations of language, that is, features common to all languages, and have noted: (1) that all children begin to talk about the same age; (2) that all have learned the basic grammar of their language by approximately the same age (usually about the age of 5); (3) that all normal children learn language merely by being exposed to it without being taught formally or conditioned to speak it; (4) that all languages and dialects are capable of expressing the universal logical operations which are the basis for cognitive functionings; and (5) that from a linguistic point of view, no language or dialect is inherently inferior to any other in its potential communicative efficiency.

These common features of language and language acquisition provide the basis for the discussion of language, learning, and cultural differences to be discussed in Chapter 4.

RECOMMENDED READING

Kolata, G. B.: The demise of the Neanderthals: Was language a factor? *Science, 186:*618, 1974.

Macnamara, J.: Cognitive basis of language learning in infants. *Psychological Review, 79*(1):1, 1972.

CHAPTER 4 PRINCIPLES OF LANGUAGE LEARNING AND CULTURAL DIFFERENCES IN LANGUAGE LEARNING

From the child of five to myself is but a step. But from the new-born baby to the child of five is an appalling distance.

TOLSTOI

SOME LEARNING PRINCIPLES

AS WE HAVE SEEN in Chapter 3, a child learns language in a social context. The rate that the child learns language is dependent upon the richness of the experiences he has had in his home and the effectiveness of his mother as a teacher. Piaget, Dewey, and Vygotsky all have suggested essentially that the opportunity for a child to interact with the environment through exploration and play encourages cognitive development. From what we have stated, the reader will realize why we stress the importance of cognitive development, for we believe that language develops under the control of and always behind cognitive development.

Recently, Condon and Sander (1974a, b) found that one- and two-day-old babies could be observed matching their thrashing movements to the rhythmic pattern of their mothers' speech. In a carefully controlled study, Condon and Sander took photographs of babies' wrists and ankles while their mothers were talking to them. They matched each baby's thrashing rhythms to those of the voice graphs of the mother's speech and found the patterns to be similar for baby and mother but different from mother to mother. If these results are found to be true universally, one can appreciate how early language learning begins in all cultures, subcultures, and families. What an enormous task it must be to try to modify a child's language after five years of learning and practice! As we saw earlier in Chapter 3, by five the child has mastered most of the phonology and morphology of his language. In addition, he has mastered a grammar unique to his cultural subgroup. Contrary to former beliefs, all children continue to master the more complex forms of English after the age of five. As we have stated, double consonants in medial positions, such as "twelfth," continue to pose problems until the child is approximately eight, and in some cases, until adulthood. Further, Piaget (1955), Sinclair-de Zwart (1973), and the cognitive linguists (see T. E. Moore, 1973) have pointed out that language acquisition is a product of cognitive acquisition. Language follows the path of cognitive development rather than precedes it. Thus, the more complex forms of logic and grammar are not mastered by the child until eight to twelve years of age. Anglin (1970) has postulated that some forms, particularly abstract relationships, are acquired after the child is twelve and are not fully mastered until adulthood. Examples of such logical constructions are *if-then, either-or,* and abstract relations which are found in the function words of *while, because, then,* and *but.* Thus, too often children who speak a different vernacular are perceived to be lower developmentally than they actually are. Their so-called lower status may be on dimensions all children have difficulty with. Let's pause a minute and consider what is known about learning and memory.

Children (and adults) try to make sense out of the world. This trying to make sense out of things is probably the basic motive force for all learning. Children build up an internalized view (or theory) of the world which we call long-term memory (Smith, 1970). It is known that children will respond to what they partially recognize and are attracted to something because it almost makes sense or is novel (Kagan, 1967). Thus, novelty and the child's involvement are crucial aspects of curriculum for young children.

Educational psychology has been based on inappropriate notions of how humans learn and these notions have not been compatible with the prevailing philosophy of education, which is largely derived from Dewey. Kohlberg (1971) states it well:

> There were a number of reasons why the Dewey revolution— what Cremin (1961) called the transformation of the schools— never became a revolution or a transformation: One was that the revolution presupposed a developmental educational psychology that Dewey had laid out in broad philosophic terms but had not filled in empirically; another was that American educational psychology went a different route, that of Thorndike, and ignored the whole concept of development. Empirical psychology was of no use to the American progressive movement of the thirties, which Dewey had started, because there was no fit between educational psychology's tests and measurements, its studies of methods of teaching and learning, and the educational philosophy of John Dewey. Thorndikean educational psychology is a blind alley for educators, partly for reasons of empirical psychology, and partly because it is based on value; premises that are philosophically unsound. Piaget's work in developmental psychology forms the basis for a new kind of educational psychology, even down to tests and measurements and testing methods, which, when integrated with the only viable philosophy of education we have—John Dewey's—offers a new meaning to schooling in America. (p. 2)

One reason Piaget's theory is so comfortable to American educational thought is that its roots reside in a common philosophical base. Claparede, Piaget's teacher and the founder of the Geneva Institute which Piaget now heads, was greatly influenced by John Dewey. Thus, Dewey's basic notion of a developmental theory of action, based on the child's interaction with the environment, i.e. Dewey's "learning by experimenting and thinking," can easily be translated into Piaget's view of the child as constructing his own intelligence through interaction with the environment. Interestingly, the line of connected thought does not stop with American education but can be found in Soviet early-childhood practice. Vygotsky (1962), an early reader of Piaget, found in him compatible notions of using play and everyday experiences as the bases of early learning.

It should be made clear at the start that Piaget's theory is a theory of cognition or thought. He does not deny the importance of personality development and a healthy self-concept; in fact, he assumes that a positive climate in which the child grows is prerequisite to learning (Piaget & Inhelder, 1969). Piaget's theory is both an age-dependent and age-independent theory. It is age-dependent in that Piaget speculates that there are general age-periods in which children become able to perform certain tasks.

The first of these periods is called the sensorimotor period, which covers the first few months of a child's life. The infant is born with four basic survival capacities: the ability to suck; the ability to turn his head, to prevent suffocation; the ability to thrash, to maintain temperature control; and the ability to process information. To Piaget, the brain's primary purpose is a survival one. The brain enables the individual to deal with the real world. Thus, from the very first days of life the young child tries to construct meaning out of what is going on around him. Piaget speculates that the child does this by two age-independent processes.

The first process he calls assimilation, which is the process by which the child "takes in" objects, ideas, or colors by constructing schemas that give these objects meaning. At first, the child builds up sets of independent schemas—that is, he is unable to relate them to each other as is characteristic of more mature thought. The young child, to Piaget, develops his first thinking through motor actions by which he can recognize objects, such as his bottle. The importance of this period is that the development of the fundamental groundwork of thinking is nonverbal in nature.

The second process the child has available to him to develop thinking Piaget calls accommodation. Accommodation is that process whereby a new structure is developed when the child is confronted with information that does not match what he already knows. For example, a child around three or four months of age comes to learn that speech sounds contain meaning. He has processed sounds since his first days, but by three or four months he is able to differentiate speech from all other sounds in the environment. Similarly, around eight months of age the child comes to recognize his parents' faces from all other faces.

The previously friendly child who smiled at everyone suddenly begins to cry in the presence of strangers. He reacts this way because he can now recognize the stranger from the nonstranger. Through the process of accommodation the child has come to reorganize faces into two specific sets—knowns and unknowns.

Piaget postulated that from birth to two years of age the child constructs all of the cognitive substructures which will later serve as the bases of thought and perceptual development. The threshold of intelligence, as intelligence is usually defined by adults, is around four and one-half months. Children begin to note constancy of size and form, but although constancy begins at age six months, the ability to accurately predict size, shape, color, and form constancy is not mature until the age of ten to twelve years.

The second age-dependent major period is preconceptual thought, which lasts approximately from two to seven years of age. Speech begins, the child learns names of objects and rapidly begins to acquire concepts. The preconceptual thinking period might best be characterized by an example used by Flavell (1963): A three-year-old child is walking in the woods with his father. He sees a rabbit; ten minutes later he sees another rabbit. To the three-year-old, both rabbits are the same rabbit rather than different objects in the same set.

The child's major means of continuing his cognitive development is through play. Piaget sees the child mastering concepts through imitation, symbolic play, drawing, construction of mental images, and finally, through the use of language to recall or categorize events.

To Piaget, the child's development of language facilitates his cognitive development. The use of language has definite advantages over sensorimotor thought in that language used in thought is much faster, can represent all of a concept at once and can deal with notions of time and space. As the child acquires language, Piaget insists that his language is only as mature as his cognitive development. To Piaget, the child acquires language by using his basic thought processes. During the preconceptual period, Piaget proposes that the child masters the names of concepts through direct experience with objects, but it is only after the five- to seven-year-old period that the child can use concepts as an organized system in thought. The seven- to eleven-year-old child can deal with numbers, relations, classes, reversibility, associativity, and identity. He cannot, however, deal with abstract thought or the calculus of proportions—such as *either-or* or *if-then* relationships.

The adolescent takes the first major step toward modes of adult thinking by acquiring the capacity of abstract thought. Piaget suggests that it is only at this stage of development that an individual can fully deal with the hypothetic-deductive reasoning typical of the research scientist.

In summary, Piaget suggests a theory of development that is hierarchical in nature and in which the child is perceived as consistently moving toward more and more mature modes of thinking. As the child masters more mature modes of thought, he is able to handle more mature forms of language.

Piaget's theory—which Piaget himself perceives as a source of hypotheses and not complete to date—is compatible with the data on brain research, particularly the development of logic and the properties of the dominant (usually the left) hemisphere of the brain (Sperry, 1968).

To Piaget and Inhelder, learning is the interaction of the child upon the environment where maturation and environment contribute to but cannot account for learning (Piaget & Inhelder, 1969). The result is that, to Piaget, the child creates his own intelligence by the process of transforming his early forms of thinking through experiences and maturation. Thus, the aim of education, whether it is done by the parent or the teacher who is cognitively-developmentally oriented, is to provide stimulation to the child for the next stage of development (Kohlberg, 1971).

It is known that one of the major principles of learning is that before something can be stored in long-term memory it must be understood. That is, a child or adult must be able to recognize, identify, or, in Piaget's terms, accommodate a new item before it can be stored in long-term memory. If something new is presented to us which has no recognizable features, our common response is not to see or hear it. Norman (1969) discusses issues of memory very well, and we recommend his book for further extension, as well as the work of Huey (1968), Bartlett (1932) and Frank Smith (1971). One example will help make the point: Most of us have experienced what we call the "cocktail party phenomenon." That is, in a crowded room filled with noise and confusion we suddenly can recognize (or hear) our name being spoken, or hear part of a conversation concerning a movie we have just seen or a book we have just read. It is as if our brains were monitoring everything that is going on, and when something that has meaning to us occurs, we suddenly hear it. Another common example is what we call the "new word phenomenon." Have you noticed that once you learn a new word for the first time how frequently you see the word in the next several days? The word has not suddenly become popular in use; it was always there. But we do not perceive what we do not know.

When confronted with the problem of learning something meaningless, humans have invented techniques to make it possible to learn them. Drill and practice are excellent devices for remembering meaningless material, for example, your social security number. Another device in aiding memory is called mnemonics, whereby to aid recall, you construct some meaning for something that is meaningless. For example, there is nothing logical about the order of the names of planets as they progress in distance from the sun. Constructing a simple sentence such as "Mary's violet eyes make John sit up nights, period" aids recall of the order—Mercury, Venus, Earth, Mars, Jupiter, Saturn, Uranus, Neptune, Pluto. The main technique in remembering meaningless material is to recall the first item and the rest flows out. However, drill and practice are not so useful for storing·information needed for problem solving or thinking, due to the fact that in drill and practice, in order to remember one part, the entire sequence must be recalled. Are there any of you readers who must still repeat the entire alphabet to determine which letter is before or after the letter "q"? If so, it is not a faulty condition of the learner but the result of a drill and practice technique used earlier in life to master the sequence of the alphabet, which is arbitrary and meaningless.

NEW LEARNING OR EXTINCTION

Some of the basic work of Skinner (1957) has proposed that once we learn something we never forget it. As Norman (1969) and Smith (1971) suggest, the more easily we learn something, the easier it is to recall it. The opposite is also true: The more difficult it is to learn something, the more difficult it is to recall. However, once learned it can always be recalled and apparently never disappears, as long as the brain remains healthy and does not suffer injury or negative effects from aging.

What is unique about learning is that, although it may seem as if some of our behaviors have disappeared, under certain conditions they will reappear full-bloom. For example, many parents have experienced moving from one section of the country to another. If the new home is located in an area of marked dialectical contrast, young children, particularly below the age of ten, will usually adopt the regional dialect quickly. Parents sometimes feel the child is "putting on" the dialect and will reprimand or tease the child about his use. The parent is often reinforced in believing the child is "faking it" because, when confronted, the child will usually angrily deny the fact, using in the course of his denial the dialect he possessed before. The importance of this anecdote is that under conditions of intense emotional experiences such as anger, fear, or grief, we usually resort to behaviors we expressed early in our life and often have not used for years. The language we learn in our family setting is with us forever, we never lose it. We can learn a new vernacular, a new language, a new mode of expression—but these new modes do not replace our original; they merely accompany it.

In terms of behavioral psychology, the explanation for this phenomenon is that when a pattern of behavior is punished or not rewarded it tends to diminish the probability of its occurrence. Once, however, the old behavior is rewarded, it will reappear.

Therefore, children's language learning is an acquisition process which operates according to the same principles as all other learning. Let's examine some of these principles.

Imitation is a powerful learning device. To some learning theorists it is perceived as the most powerful (Bandura, 1969). Certainly we can all observe a great deal of imitative learning in children in such things as their walk, speech patterns and dress.

Modeling, while similar to imitation, is somewhat different. Modeling is more the conscious acquisition in a general way of a particular behavior of another—for instance, boys doing culturally approved masculine things but not necessarily in direct imitation of the father. As an example, Rau, Anastasiow, and Mlodnosky (1963) found that fathers who showed high interest in watching sports on TV tended to have boys who preferred to play with culturally designated male toys. The boys did not necessarily watch sports on TV but displayed modeling behavior of an associated masculine type.

Children appear to utilize both imitation and modeling in language learning. As they develop they can be heard making closer and closer approximations to the speech patterns of their parents, so that the vernacular of the home becomes the vernacular of the child.

Parents' use of reward as a child comes closer to current pronunciation or identification of a word is another powerful learning strategy. Punishment is very effective in reducing the probability of a behavior occurring, whereas reward increases the occurrence of a desired behavior.

Replacement refers to the offering of a substitute behavior for one the parent or society finds undesirable. Experienced first-grade teachers frequently offer a wide range of attractive choices when a child finishes assigned work. These choices are to serve two purposes: One, as a reward for finishing assigned work; and two, to provide the child with acceptable alternatives to other behaviors which are not acceptable. For example, it may be all right to work quietly on a puzzle, whereas talking, running, or wrestling are unacceptable behaviors.

As we mentioned in Chapter 1, parents who set achievement standards and use reasoning and the teaching technique of reward usually have children who are more successful in school. The goal of doing well in school is largely a middle-class one, which some members of the lower-class accept. As Basil Bernstein (1972) points out, the language of the middle-class encourages the acquisition of many kinds of skills. One set of skills which is taught has to do with attitudes and values usually thought of as a "moral code." Middle-class parents not only prepare their children for school by encouraging acquisition of learning styles that are compatible with those desired by teachers (Mlodnosky, 1963; Anastasiow, 1963) and that are conducive to achieving the goals of the school; but the *hidden curriculum* of the home (Deutsch, 1965) also includes attitudes and values related to how one behaves and what one prizes. One of the authors, in interviewing second graders and asking why it was important to do well in school, remembers clearly a seven-year-old's response that unless you did well in second grade you would not be able to go to college. As Bernstein elaborates, the code of the middle-class parent is more than academically oriented; it is universalistically oriented. That is, middle-class parents tend to generalize about behavior such as "Good boys don't do that" or "All good boys want to please their mothers." Lower social-class parents, according to Bernstein, tend to "particularize events." The lower-class parent usually states explanations in the form of commands rather than in terms of cause and effect. The joker in the whole training model, to Bernstein, is that the schools are based on the same "universalistic code" of the middle-class, and lower socioeconomic status (SES) students have not had experience in dealing with language used in this way. To Bernstein, if the school is to be successful and wants the culture of the teacher to become part of the consciousness of the child, the culture of the child must first be in the consciousness of the teacher.

As the lower SES child learns his language, he also learns values and attitudes concerning behavior, which are embedded within the universalistic code. These attitudes reflect the basic Puritan ethic which most middle-class Westerners share and which includes, among others, such values as cleanliness, thrift, hard work, honesty, denial of immediate gratification, and the acceptance of a moral purpose to live. The Greek and Jewish immigrant shared values similar to those of the Puritan ethic, and it should be no surprise that these two groups made an easier transition into the American society than some other ethnic groups. Similarly, the rapidity with which the Japanese have been able to make an adjustment to the Western culture may be found in the similarities between the Tokugawa and Puritan ethics (Werner, et al., 1971).

Most people tend to speak to their young child in simple sentences (Snow, 1972). Mothers tend to use speech styles which contain more redundancies and amplify what the child has said. For example, if a child has said, "Doggie," the mother probably will reply with, "Yes, Doggie," "Good Doggie," "See the Doggie."

There are major differences between the teaching styles of middle-class mothers and many, though not all, lower-class parents. Many lower-class parents tend not to amplify or expand upon the child's spoken language and are limited in their verbal interactions with their children. These findings have been demonstrated by a number of researchers (Chilman, 1966; Hess & Shipman, 1965; Olim, 1970; Bee et al., 1962; Cazden, 1974). Cazden makes a strong point of the need for the parent to encourage children's play with language. Children naturally experiment with sounds, and many children will practice and play with sounds in their crib just before falling asleep (Weir, 1962).

Those children who make the easiest adjustment in school and have a smooth introduction to learning to read, usually have mothers who have used expression in their speech, tried to understand what their child is saying, encouraged the child to *play* with language (sillie, nillie, Willy, Billy, hilly, etc.), and provided models of language with strong overcorrection.

Many lower-class mothers do not use these techniques. What this may mean for teachers is that, while the child may be capable enough, he has not had the language experiences related to school success. Too often we judge a child to be unintelligent due to his lack of *experience* with language. This is a serious error. Schools must accommodate to the needs of the youngster; for if children have not had these experiences, school failure is predictable unless the schools provide many language experiences before introducing formal reading.

SUMMARY

In this chapter we have proposed that the differences among social and ethnic groups are not a simple matter of language differences. We have suggested that if success in schools is used as a criterion of success in life, then the middle-class parent usually does a number of things that enhance the probability of his child's success. Middle-class parents tend to use effective learning strategies. These same parents also tend to teach motivational patterns of achievement that are very similar to those used by the school. In addition, middle-class parents teach values that are consonant with the dominant cultural value, that is, the Puritan ethic. Embedded in the language the middle-class child is taught to use are concepts and understandings reflecting the universalistic code of the middle-class. Finally, the vernacular used in the lower socioeconomic family not only contains some different phonological and morphological features, but also contains a different grammar. These language differences will be examined in the next chapter.

RECOMMENDED READING

Hobbs, N.: *The Futures of Children.* San Francisco, Jossey-Bass, 1975.
Bijou, S. W., and Baer, D. W.: *Child Development I: A Systematic and Empirical Theory.* New York, Appleton-Century-Crofts, 1961.
Gordon, I. J.: *The Infant Experience.* Columbus, Merrill, 1975.

CHAPTER 5 MEASURING SUBCULTURAL LANGUAGE DIFFERENCES

"It ain't what you say, it's the way that you say it."

IT IS HOPED the reader now has a conception of the context of how vernaculars develop and the legitimacy of a given vernacular to serve a linguistic community. Douglas Gordon, a linguist, said at a recent conference in reference to Standard English, "standard is what the ear will tolerate." The point Gordon was making is that what the culture considers as *standard* is what the adult has come to accept as socially proper and therefore acceptable. There are vast regional dialects existing currently in the United States, which vary largely on a geographical base. In some cases the vernacular or dialect has developed because of the geographical isolation of the particular community. In other cases it has developed due to the group's original ethnic background. These vernaculars are variants of Standard English, in both sound and grammar. They include the New England speech —as exemplified by a former U.S. president of the early 1960's— the soft, broad drawl of the Southeastern Midlands or the so-called cultured Southern speech, the "twang" of the Midwest, the Appalachian Elizabethan structure, and the social dialects of the Mexican-American, American Indian, American black, Puerto Rican, Hawaiian, Oriental, and Portuguese Americans who reside in Hawaii. What "grate" on the ear are not just phonological or morphological differences but grammatical differences which are also a part of the vernacular of lower-class ethnic groups. Children from lower socioeconomic classes generally do not do as well in school as middle-class children, and vernaculars and dialects are often cited as the cause of school failure, particularly in learning how to read.

In the next chapter, we will describe our original work with children who reside in poverty and our interpretation of these children's so-called language problems. Following that, we will discuss our more recent studies and their results. In subsequent chapters we will make some suggestions based on these results as to how a lower SES culturally different child might be helped to succeed in the middle-class-oriented school.

REJECTION OF "POOR" ENGLISH

The term "poor English" has been with us for a long time. It has a double meaning. One, it is language spoken by the economically poor; and two, it is poor, meaning bad, less sophisticated, and, most damning of all, a supposed reflection of lower intelligence. Most middle-class Americans perceive the person who speaks "bad" grammar as being mentally retarded. Speaking and writing language well (not legibility) are major demands made by the agents of the school and the culture at large for school success and employment into major white-collar positions. The term "poor English" also has another subtle distinction; it is a speaker's means of hiding his racial rejections of the ethnically different speaker. For the immigrant of the late 1800's and early 1900's, accent and grammar were perceived as socially relevant means for limiting occupational employment. Rather than saying, "We do not hire Italians, Greeks, Jews" and so on, the rejection was based on the immigrant's accent or "poor English." As second and third generation children became able to master "Standard" English, the white child could pass into the mainstream of American society. However, the Oriental, Mexican-American, Atlantic Islanders, and particularly the black could not pass due to color biases. It should be recognized that rejection of some vernaculars is at times a guise for rejecting ethnic minorities Mercer (1973) has ample evidence to demonstrate that the preponderance of black and Mexican-American children who are in special education classes are there for other than academic lacks

Guskin (1970) has shown that when asked to rate tape recordings of identical conversations about a child's very real anxieties one spoken by a black child and the other by a white child, teachers rated the black child as being a "serious problem," "one probably not too intelligent," "violent," or "ugly," whereas they rated the white middle-class child as probably being a product of a broken home or some other factor outside the child. Teachers in Guskin's study frequently expressed empathy for the white child, saying they felt sorry for him. No such sentiments were expressed for the black child. McDonald (1971) found in a study of stereotypes of speech, which included "white Northerners," "black Northerners," "white Southerners" and "black Southerners," that black was rated lower than white in the North, and Southern was consistently rated lower, with "black Southern" lowest of all. Naremore (1969) collected similar findings when she had teachers rate transcribed interviews of black and white children. Both black and white teachers in Naremore's study rated black children lower on a variety of dimensions. Naremore, Guskin, and McDonald in each of their separate studies concluded that the lower rating of black children is due to more than just dialect. In each of their studies they feel that the data justify assuming that when the dialect signifies blackness to the rater, the rater will judge blackness as inferior. These attitudes are very difficult to change and, as McDonald reports in her study, may be impervious to direct educational measures.

How then can it be determined that the language of the five-year-old is adequate for school success, particularly when the child speaks a subcultural vernacular?

PROBLEMS OF ASSESSING LANGUAGE DEVELOPMENT OF LOWER SES CHILDREN

In our initial work with black and white lower SES children, we were confronted with the problem of determining at what level of cognitive or language development the children were functioning. Their styles of language were different from ours, and our ears were not attuned to their speech. Another major problem confronts the research worker who attempts to gather a language sample of the child who resides in poverty or who is from a different ethnic group: These children are not motivated toward a testing situation. They do not realize that the school expects children to do as well as they can when given adult requests to perform. Ginsburg (1972) has mentioned this as one of the major fallacies underlying IQ test scores with lower SES children. An IQ score assumes the child was motivated to do well on the test. Most lower SES children, when they first come to school, do not understand the word "test," or its euphemism "play a game," as meaning a time when they are to do their best.

Loban (1963) in his work in California was successful in getting speech samples by asking children questions. Most of the questions had to do with the children's experiences. In a research project in California, Anastasiow (1965b) was able to collect language samples with five-year-old middle-class children. From these data it was possible to score the samples on articulation and spontaneous verbal fluency, two measures which were excellent predictors in the subsequent reading study. In the earlier study it was found that 75 percent of all reading problems at the end of first grade could have been identified at the beginning of the year by a child's low spontaneous verbal fluency scores. As stressed by Anastasiow (1971) in a previous paper, oral language is an aspect of thought, and verbal fluency can be used to approximate the level of language usage development of the child.

As we have pointed out, the poverty child may present some unique instructional problems for the classroom teacher, especially in assessing level of developmental growth. The need for a classroom assessment instrument for oral language became apparent in our work with poverty children who generally speak a nonstandard vernacular and were reluctant to respond spontaneously. The practical problem of acquiring a valid and reliable sample of a child's language was a primary emphasis in our work. An important aspect of the task that was developed is the sampling technique used and the general applicability of that technique to a wide variety of situations and content. In order to more fully understand the advantages and disadvantages of the sentence repetition technique, a variety of other means for obtaining language samples will be discussed.

Perhaps the most common means of assessing a child's language is spontaneous speech sampling. Menyuk (1968a) suggested that spontaneous speech sampling is among the easier techniques for obtaining valid information about a child's knowledge of language. The technique involves tape recording or manually recording whatever the child says verbally within a given length of time. In most cases, no restraints are placed on the child, and he is allowed to move about freely in the environment. While no other technique can claim the validity of spontaneous speech sampling, the obvious problem of reliability is perhaps more disturbing. Spontaneous speech samples are valid to the extent that no artificial conditions are imposed on the child and his use of language. However, they may be unreliable since it is virtually impossible to reproduce the conditions under which a particular sample was gathered.

Spontaneous speech sampling is perhaps best suited for gathering specific kinds of diagnostic information, such as the use of verb forms or vocabulary. An observant teacher can learn a great deal about the language knowledge of children by recording and analyzing the speech produced in the classroom.

Grammatical closure is another procedure for obtaining language samples. This technique builds on the validity of spontaneous speech sampling, but increases reliability by structuring the situation from which the sample is obtained. Grammatical closure, or sentence completion, is a rather common procedure in which a portion of a sentence is given and the child is asked to complete the sentence. Depending on the specific aim of the investigator, the given portion of the sentence will vary in length and complexity. The well-known Berko Test (1958) is a highly structured form of grammatical closure. Berko was interested in children's knowledge of morphological rules and children's ability to apply those rules to new cases. For example, a child may be shown a picture of a fictional creature and told "This is a wug." When presented with a picture showing two of the creatures, the child is asked to complete the sentence, "Here are two . . . . ." If the child appropriately responds with "wugs" the investigator can make an inference about the child's knowledge of morphological rules.

Piaget (1955) used a less structured procedure and asked children to complete sentences which had been given and which ended in "because" and other similar connectives. Piaget's approach allowed for more spontaneous responses, which can be difficult to analyze when making comparisons between samples. For example, at one point in time a child may respond minimally, while at another time, quite elaborately, depending on the environment. Thus, the grammatical closure technique, when minimally structured, faces the same difficulties as spontaneous speech sampling; namely, the amount and complexity of response may be a function of the environment and not necessarily reflective of the child's potential language output.

A third technique frequently used in the classroom for instruction and assessment purposes is story dictation. Many teachers will ask children to produce stories on a weekly basis. While each child will undoubtedly develop a story based on his particular experience, the teacher can apply analytical procedures to the story much as she would to a sample of spontaneous speech. The advantage of the story dictation procedure is that each child is requested to produce connected discourse. That is, each child begins the procedure with some structure which will minimally interfere with the language output. Spontaneous speech sampling imposes no structure on the language output, while the grammatical closure technique may strictly focus the language output for the child.

Many rural poverty children have low spontaneous verbal-fluency scores. Typically, when a child is asked what he does on Saturday morning, the interview dialogue will go something like this:

Interviewer: What do you do on Saturday morning?
Child: Watch TV.
Interviewer: What do you watch on TV?
Child: Popeye.
Interviewer: Can you tell me about the program?
Child: Yeah!
Interviewer: Will you tell me about the program?
Child: There's Olive Oyl.
Interviewer: Yes?
Child: There's Brutus.
... and so on.

Our experiences have led us to expect one- or two-word responses. Yet these same children can be observed on the playground talking rapidly, spontaneously, and obviously with a great deal of communicative skills.

In addition to the failure of many investigators to collect samples of spontaneous speech from poverty children, we suspected that low scores on the initial administration of the Peabody Picture Vocabulary Test and Illinois Test of Psycholinguistic Abilities (ITPA) are due in part to the poverty child's failure to learn an appropriate set in test-taking behavior, rather than to the child's lack of ability. In our opinion, some research workers of the early 1960's who set up programs for children residing in poverty made erroneous assumptions as to a child's level of language competency based on the child's tendency not to respond (*see* particularly Bereiter & Engleman's (1966) early assumptions and Labov's (1972) critique of Bereiter & Engleman). For example, some researchers assumed that the children failed to develop language due to the fact that these children resided in noisy homes where the signal-to-noise ratio made it difficult for the child to understand what was being said (Deutsch, 1964). Unfortunately, some of these assumptions once written into the literature remain as *truths* way beyond the time when data are available to challenge them.

Labov (1972) found black lower SES teenagers to possess a rich verbal language in social situations, and one of the authors of this text found that black rural lower SES kindergarten and first grade children would dictate rich and involved stories in response to their art work (Anastasiow, 1971). Butterfield and Zigler (1965) also found that if the poverty child was given opportunity to learn that test-taking behaviors are important and given time to establish rapport, statistically significant scores could be obtained. In summary, part of a lower SES child's supposed language deficit or handicap is based on his low scores obtained on measures where the assumption is that the child recognizes he is taking a test and is motivated to do well.

THE SENTENCE REPETITION TASK

One technique that linguists have constructed to determine the level of language development of middle-class children is the so-called repeated sentence technique. This technique is based on the findings that children acquire the same linguistic structures at about the same age. In addition, the technique assumes that in order to hear and repeat a sentence, the child must have acquired the particular form in the language and be able to understand it. This is a cognitive point of view and was discussed in the last chapter. Menyuk (1971), in a series of studies, was able to show that children, when asked to repeat simple sentences, would omit portions of the sentence that were beyond their level of language development. That is, the child would repeat the sentence leaving out that portion that was beyond his cognitive or language maturity. After Menyuk's initial work, many other linguists developed the technique further, documenting the basic premises underlying the assumption of the instrument. (*See* Slobin (1967) for an excellent summary of the instruments and studies.) From Menyuk's and Slobin's work, we speculated that the omission scores could be used as an indication of potential developmental delay. For example, most children of a chronological age of five have mastered the irreversible passive; therefore, when a child omitted the passive from a sentence he was asked to repeat, we felt it could be assumed that the child had not yet mastered that aspect of language. Thus, we perceived that one purpose the repeated sentence technique could serve would be as an assessment of a child's language acquisition regardless of the dialect he speaks. Some preliminary studies prior to ours led us to explore the possibility. For example, other linguists saw the technique as a means of demonstrating the language facility of the child who speaks a different vernacular. Baratz (1973) was able to show that black children were superior to white children in repeating sentences spoken in dialect, whereas white children were superior to black children in repeating standard vernacular. Baratz and Shuy (1969) report other studies which have similar findings.

Thus, our studies were based on the following assumptions:

1. Children would omit from sentences they were asked to repeat those portions that were beyond their level of development. This score is called *function word omissions*.

2. Children who were asked to repeat sentences would change

portions of the sentence to conform to their own dialect. This score we have called *reconstructions*.

THE SENTENCE REPETITION TASK (SRT) AS A MEASURE OF LANGUAGE USAGE

Given the assumptions above, we hypothesized that the SRT could be used to gather support for the position that lower SES children who speak a different vernacular are normal in intellectual functioning. That is, we proposed that if black, Puerto Rican, and lower-class white children were asked to repeat well-constructed Standard English sentences, they would do so as well as white middle-class children. However, we suspected that these children would repeat the sentences as they would say them in their own vernacular, rather than in the way the sentences were spoken to them. Said in another way, we anticipated that these children would *reconstruct* portions of the sentences given in Standard English that had an equivalent form in their own vernacular. We believed that if the child were able to *reconstruct* to appropriate forms in his own vernacular, this act (or behavior) could be interpreted as a sign of normal cognitive functioning. For example, if the child was asked to repeat the sentence "He was hit" and said, "He got hit," we interpreted this feat to indicate the child's ability to change the sentence to conform not only to his own dialect, while maintaining the essential meaning of the sentence, but also to change it to an appropriate form in his own vernacular. (He didn't say, "He is hit," a construction used infrequently in that particular sentence form.) This aspect of language usage will be discussed in more detail in Chapter 6.

As a second major use of the SRT, we perceived that by administering the SRT to a group of young children who speak a different dialect, we would be able to differentiate those students who fall within the normal range of language and cognitive development (high reconstructers) from those who may be developmentally delayed (high omitters). In addition, we hoped to demonstrate that children who speak a different vernacular are as able as middle-class children in repeating function words. We approached this problem from the reverse. Too often everything a child cannot do is assumed to be a product of the child's inability rather than due to his level of development. For example, handicapped children are frequently misjudged as being slow in some aspect of their development because of their handicapped condition (blindness, deafness, etc.); whereas in fact their inability may be age-associated, and normal children of similar ages may not possess the same skill. It was predicted that the same phenomenon would be demonstrable for children who speak a different vernacular. Drawing upon the work of Neisser (1967), Lenneberg (1967), and Piaget (1955), we predicted that most children of ages five through eight would have difficulty with sentences that reflected abstract thinking forms typical of an older child. We drew upon Piaget's theory and suggested that forms such as *if-then* and *either-or* reflect cognitive abilities not mastered by most children until ten to twelve years of age, the period of abstract reasoning. From Neisser, we evolved that some function words reflect qualities whose abstractness appears to be of the nature that would not be mastered until Piaget's period of abstract reasoning—such as *while*. We expected that black, white poverty, and white middle-class children would have high omission scores in sentences that contained these forms, demonstrating the similarity of the children's cognitive development. Our analysis of the acquisition of function words is discussed in more detail in Chapter 7.

Thus, with an emphasis on measuring dialect usage and general language development, sentences were constructed to:

1. reflect most forms of middle-class Standard English;
2. have words which have equivalent forms in lower SES vernacular;
3. have a form which would be omitted by most five- to eight-year-olds.

Our initial studies had several primary purposes:

1. To develop an instrument to help kindergarten and Head Start teachers distinguish children of normal development from those of delayed development.
2. To support the cognitive-language difference hypothesis

rather than the genetic deficit hypothesis for children who speak a different vernacular.

3. To develop a list of forms lower SES children use in their common responses to Standard English forms.

Since the Anastasiow/Hanes SRT was developed to measure two rather complex aspects of language usage—dialect usage and function word acquisition—each topic is discussed fully in separate chapters. Chapter 6 deals directly with children's subcultural dialect and suggests how teachers and/or researchers can determine children's language usage. Chapter 7 deals with children's ability to handle function words and discusses, thereby, how an estimate of a child's cognitive functioning may be made somewhat free of cultural bias.

ADDITIONAL READING

Gupta, W., and Stern, C.: Comparative effectiveness of speaking vs. listening in improving spoken language of disadvantaged young children. *Journal of Experimental Education,* 38(1):54, 1969.

Mitchell I., Rosanoff, I. R., and Rosanoff, A. J.: A study of association in Negro children. *Psychological Review, 26*:354, 1919.

Venezky, R. L.: Nonstandard language and reading. *Elementary English,* 47(3):334, 1970.

Samuda, R. J.: *Psychological Testing of American Minorities.* New York, Dodd, Mead, and Co., 1975.

Seitz, V.: Integrated versus segregated school attendance and immediate recall for standard and nonstandard English. *Developmental Psychology* (in press).

Wolfram, W.: Selected bibliographies: (1) Textbooks and readers in sociolinguistics. *The Linguistic Reporter,* September, 1973.

Wolfram, W.: Selected bibliographies: (2) Textbooks and readers in the sociology of language. *The Linguistic Reporter,* November, 1973.

Center for Applied Linguistics. An annotated bibliography on black language for teachers. Author, 1971.

CHAPTER 6 RECONSTRUCTIONS

When one masters one's language, you understand the
world as others see it.

THE BASIC IDEA expressed above is key to understanding the notions presented in this chapter. Humans, when learning something new, try to translate the new information into terms, ideas,
or analogies of what they already know. If it is a word, we seek
a known synonym; if it is an idea, we may seek a known analogy,
simile, or metaphor. For example, poets use the technique frequently of seeking an experience familiar to the reader to describe an insight the poet has just arrived at, as a black adult is
quoted as saying in reference to dealing with whites, "You have
to be so careful it's as if you were stepping between raindrops"
(Cazden, John & Hymes, 1972).

The basic notion of translating a perceived object into a
known description is a common behavior. Basically, reconstruction is a similar process. It is the process of receiving a message
and repeating that message into the dialect of the speaker. In the
example used in Chapter 1, a black child is asked to repeat the
sentence "I asked him if he did it and he said he didn't do it,"
and says: "I asks him if he did it and he says he didn't did it."
The message is the same, but the form of the repeated sentence
has been reconstructed by the child to conform to the regulari-
ties of the dialect he has learned at home.

If, as we have stated in the previous chapter, children who reside in poverty develop language as other children, then why do
they talk so differently? To us, the difference is in dialect, not in
content. Our function word studies support the notion that all
normal children learn language in relation to their stage of cognitive development. Children's oral expression of language, how-

ever, varies widely based on familial, regional and national differences.

In addition, the amount of language used by a child varies from family to family and across ethnic groups and social classes. The stereotype of the *silent* American Indian has just begun to be modified. For example, Dumont (*in* Cazden, John & Hymes) points out that in the Oglala Sioux nation silence is an attribute of the classroom, not the child. The Sioux child has been socialized to speak only when he has mastered the lesson, not before. Sioux children, as black inner-city children, are noisy and talkative outside of class. It may be too broad a generalization, but both black and white rural-South families tend to encourage children not to speak in the presence of adults. Horner and Gussow (1972) demonstrate that black mothers may be more restrictive with their sons than with their daughters. The old adage "Children should be seen and not heard" appears to us to remain in operation among the lower socioeconomic groups in the United States.

Thus, we perceive that children who reside in poverty tend to speak less in the presence of adults and to remain less verbal in school. Both of these factors tend to magnify the teacher's perception that these children are "less developed verbally." It also makes it more difficult to obtain an adequate sample of the child's language. The Sentence Repetition Task solves this problem, for more than 2,000 children have readily demonstrated to us their willingness to repeat sentences even though many of these same children (black, white, Puerto Rican, Oriental, and so on) do not become easily engaged in conversation.

The first major goal of the research was to gain support for the belief that children, when asked to repeat well-formed English sentences, would change or reconstruct portions of the sentences to conform to their own vernacular. Embedded in each given sentence was a form that had an equivalent form in low SES dialect. Thus, the sentences were constructed to allow for the potential occurrence of reconstructions.

The major forms that were drawn upon were based on the

work of Baratz (1969) and Labov (1972). Their work with inner-city black children indicated that there were consistent differences between middle-class English and so-called black inner-city vernacular.

Baratz (1969) identified the common differences between black inner-city vernacular and white middle-class English.

Written	*Linguistic Feature*	*Oral Expression*
John's house	possession	John house
John runs	3rd single present	John run
ten cents	plural	ten cent
He jumped	past	He jump
She is a cook	copula	She a cook
He doesn't have any toys	negation	He ain't got no toys He don't have no toys
He asked if I came	past conditional question	He asked did I come
Everyday when I come he isn't here	negation to be	Everyday when I come he don't be here

In addition to these forms Labov (1972) reported the following phonological differences:

1. r less-ness .... guard = God
2. l less-ness .... tool = too
3. simplification of consonant clusters .... past = pass
4. weakening of final consonants .... mend = men
5. lack of /i/ and /e/ distinction
6. lack of distinction of /ih/ and /eh/ before /r/
7. /ay/ and /aw/ sounds like /ah/

Labov also indicates that inner-city speech contains a unique form which he has called the *negative attraction*. For example, "It ain't no cat can't get in no coop" translated into white middle-class English becomes: "There isn't any cat that can get into my pigeon coop."

The following charts contain the sentences that were used and the scoring key.

Sentence Repetition Task

1. He was tied up.
2. She isn't a good singer.
3. Where can he do what he wants?
4. Then he went to the movies by himself.
5. She said, 'Whose toys are those?"
6. Did an accident happen while your mother was in the store?
7. Jim, who tried to escape, was caught and then beaten up.
8. Although I want ice cream, I bet I'm not going to get any.
9. The boy was hit by the girl who jumped rope in the street.
10. He runs home quickly after school because he has a bicycle to ride.
11. If you want to see an elephant's baby, then you will have to go to a zoo.
12. Joe is good when he feels like it.
13. His mother wouldn't let him go to school because he had no shoes to wear.
14. I think Mary is absent because her mother thought she was sick.
15. The boys were given lots of milk by the ladies in the lunch room.
16. You should either say nice things to your friends or not say anything at all.
17. Joe has to be quiet in class or his teacher won't let him have recess.
18. Joe fell down the stairs while his mother talked to the baby.
19. The teacher will give you a smile when you have finished your work.
20. If your papers are neater, then your teacher will be happier.
21. She's got a lollipop which she's going to give me if I'm nice to her.
22. I asked him if he did it and he said he didn't do it.
23. What are you doing tomorrow morning after you've eaten breakfast?
24. He couldn't have any ice cream because his sister ate it all up.
25. Although Jimmy felt sick, he came to school.

26. Half of nine is not four, because four and four makes eight.
27. His mother will give him a cookie when he has eaten his supper.
28. That animal is not dead because it is still moving.

Scoring Key for Reconstruction Words

1.	was tied	got tied
2.	isn't a	ain't no; ain't a
3.	wants	want
4.	movies	movie
5.	said . . . toys	say . . . toy
6.	Did . . . mother	was . . . noun variant
7.	was caught . . . beaten up	got caught . . . got beat up; beat up; got beaten up
8.	I'm not going to	I ain't gonna; I not gonna; I'm not gonna
9.	was hit . . . jumped	got hit . . . jump, was rope jumping, was jumping rope
10.	runs . . . has	run . . . have
11.	elephant's . . . will have	baby elephant; elephant baby . . . have; got
12.	is . . . feels	be; delete . . . feel
13.	had . . . shoes	have, didn't have no . . . shoe
14.	is . . . was	be; delete . . . got
15.	boys . . . lots	boy . . . lot; alot
16.	things . . . friends	thing . . . friend
17.	has . . . have	got . . . get
18.	stairs . . . talked	stair . . . talk
19.	will give . . . you have . . . finished	be giving; give . . . you (delete have) . . . finish
20.	papers . . . will be	paper . . . be
21.	She's . . . she's . . . I'm	she got, she has got or she has . . . she going, she is going . . . I be; I
22.	if . . . said	did . . . say
23.	are . . . you've eaten	delete; be . . . you eat

24. ate	eat
25. felt ... came	feel ... come
26. is not ... makes	ain't ... make
27. will give ... he has eaten	be giving; give ... he eat
28. is not	ain't

PROCEDURES FOR ADMINISTRATION

In the sentence repetition task, the child should be asked to repeat the stimulus sentence exactly as presented. If the child does not give a complete verbatim repetition of the example sentence given in the standard instructions, the instructions including the example sentence should be repeated. We advise pre-recording the sentences. Select for your speaker a voice that is relatively free of regional dialects so that your measure is one of the child's ability to understand middle-class white vernacular. The standard instructions are:

> These machines are tape recorders. Have you ever used a tape recorder before? Would you like to tell this tape recorder your name and how old you are?

> (Replay the tape so that the child can hear his voice on the tape recorder.)

> Now we are going to play a game. To help us play this game we will use these machines (point to the two tape recorders). This machine will say some words to you (point to the large tape recorder). What I want you to do is to say *exactly* what it says, into this machine (point to the small tape recorder). For example, suppose the machine says, "The man is tall," what would you say? (If the child repeats correctly, continue; if not, repeat the example again.)

> Now, listen to what the machine says and then you say *exactly* what it says, O.K.?

Reconstruction words are
scored correct if:

1. Response stated is verbatim.
2. Response is stated twice, once verbatim, the other time wrong or reconstructed.
3. Response is contracted into a noun or pronoun (for example, "teacher'll" instead of "teacher will").

scored as a reconstruction and correct if the word or phrase:

1. Is clearly in reconstructed form as stated on scoring guide.
2. Is said twice (once reconstructed, the other incorrect).
3. Is expanded from a contraction. (For example, "she has got" instead of "she's got" or more formal English, such as "she has"; also in sentence 13 "had no" to "didn't have any"; and in sentence 21 "she's going to" to "she is going go.")

scored as an error if the reconstructed word or phrase:

1. Is an inappropriate response (not a reconstruction).
2. Is distorted beyond intelligibility.
3. In sentence 7 ("beaten up") was altered to "beat him up."
4. In sentence 9 ("jumped") was altered to "that had the rope."
5. In sentence 13 ("had"), 10 ("has"), 17 ("has, have"), and 19 ("have") was pronounced "ha . . ."
6. In sentence 11 ("will have") was altered to "won't have" or "don't have."

scored omission if function or reconstruction word or phrase:

1. Is not repeated in the response sentence.
2. If no response was made to the stimulus sentence.
3. If background noise or sound reproduction affected discriminability of the word(s).

The instrument has been administered in several settings and our findings have been very similar. For ease of interpreting, we will present the results of several different studies which serve as exemplars of our research.

In a study of white rural poverty, black inner-city poverty and white middle-class kindergarten, first, and second graders, we found that black inner-city children *reconstructed* about 68 percent of the words that had equivalents in "poverty dialect," while white rural and city groups reconstructed around 50 percent. The percentages were steady across grades (see Figure 1).

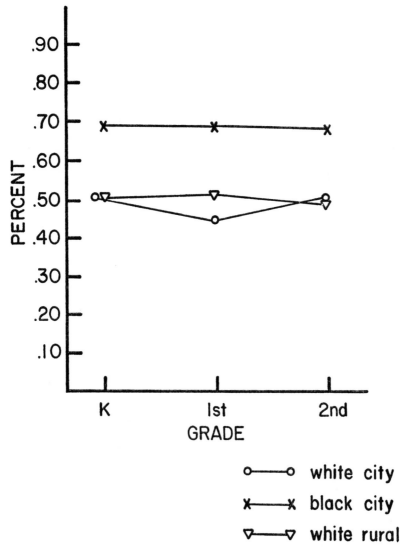

Figure 1. Proportion of Words "Reconstructed" to Total Number of Errors.

If we compare black, white, and Puerto Rican children as we did in another study, we find the following:

Mean Number of Words Reconstructed

Grade	Blacks	N	Whites	N	Puerto Rican	N
1	11.35	(100)	8.21	(104)	11.62	(47)
2	10.63	(92)	8.15	(121)	11.60	(55)
3	8.69	(26)	6.78	(94)	9.86	(36)

Although children tend to reconstruct fewer words as they advance in grade, they still reconstruct a large number of words. In another study we conducted with kindergarten through sixth grade children in a midwest inner-city, we found that at the end of fourth grade the number of reconstructions began to drop for black students. We, as yet, have no comparable data for white students but suspect the same trend.

What we are asserting is that there is a relationship between when a child begins to move from Piaget's concrete operations stage to abstract reasoning and his ability to reconstruct in oral language; and that this relationship can be observed by the child repeating more of the standard forms. It may be well into the abstract reasoning stage (junior high school) before the child adopts (if he chooses to adopt) a standard dialect in preference to the one he originally learned. Douglas Gordon, a distinguished linguist at Howard University, and John Joyner of the American Speech and Hearing Association both have stated that it is around fourteen to sixteen years of age before a teenager will "switch" dialects, *if* he is going to switch.

In analyzing each reconstruction children made, we found that many forms adhered to the dialect of lower socioeconomic dialects. However, children offered many forms which were close to the original but not syntactically correct. We labeled the latter forms errors.

In the following pages, note the kinds of reconstructions and errors each ethnic group made. Particularly note the large number of responses in sentences involving eating.

For teachers who use the SRT in the classroom as a diagnostic tool, we suggest the following:

1. Administer the sentences as described.
2. Score all "reconstruction" words.
3. Use the scoring key to determine whether the child uses a form we found to be typical.
4. In children who make a large number of "reconstructions" (over 12), plan an intensive language stimulation program in conjunction with their regular program (see the last chapter).
5. For children who make a large number of errors (over 12), delay formal reading; initiate an oral language program.
6. For children who make a large number of omissions, seek a consultant to determine the level of the child's cognitive functioning.
7. Note we have not provided norms for the test. Each child should be scored individually and compared only to the social group of which he is a member. In integrated settings, lower-class children should be compared only to lower-class children. No other comparison is legitimate.

Unique Reconstructions
Inner-city Black
(N = 210)

No.	Word	Reconstructions	Errors
1.	was tied		tied (2)
			is tied (2)
			is a
2.	isn't a	ain't a (3)	is not (2)
		is not a (3)	was tie
		ain't no (2)	is a (3)
			was a
			isn't
			is no
			was tied
			is a (3)
			no is a
3.	wants	want (65)	
4.	movies	movie (67)	

No. Word	Reconstructions	Errors
5. said	say (31)	se' (2)
	says (2)	to say
		was
		toy
toys	toy (31)	she
6. did	was there	the
	was (3)	there was
		is (2)
mother	mama (4)	you
	mommie	you were
	mom	
7. was caught	got caught (23)	caught (18)
	got caughten up	and caught (3)
		then caught
		is caught
beaten up	got beated up	was trying to beat
	beat up (21)	somebody up
	was beat up (2)	who caught
	got beat up (11)	caught (5)
	got beaten up (8)	
	got all beat up	
	get beat up (5)	
	was beaten up (7)	
	beatened up	
8. I'm not	I'm not gonna (32)	I do not want to
going to	I ain't gonna (26)	get none
	I not gonna (3)	I wasn't going
	I won't get any (15)	I not try
	I won't get	I am gonna to
	I wouldn't get	I can't get any
	I won't	I want to get (2)
	I don't get none	I want to get any
	I won't get none (6)	I gonna get any
	I wouldn't get any	but (3)
	I ain't gettin (2)	but I'm
	I won't even get any	but I better

No. Word	*Reconstructions*	*Errors*
	I wasn't going to	but I bet (2)
	get none	but I (2)
	I almost ain't gonna	
	I ain't gonna get	
	none	
	I won't get it	
9. was hit	got hit (43)	got jump
		hitted
		has been hit
		hit
		was get hit
jumped	jump (78)	was in
	jump rope	had jump
	jumpin'	was jumped
	jumping rope (2)	rollin'
	was jumping (9)	went jumping
	was jumpin' (2)	was jump (2)
	was jump rope (10)	roped
	was jumpin'	were jump
	rope (4)	jumping (6)
	was jumpin' in the	was in the street
	street (3)	by jumpin'
	who played jump	who's jump
	rope jumpin'	
	was jumping	
	rope (8)	
	jumpin' rope (3)	
10. runs	run (77)	runnèd (8)
		ride
		(distortion)
		can get
		west (3)
		rolls
has	have (71)	had (20)
	he's got	get (36)
		ride

No. Word	Reconstructions	Errors
		ha' (4)
11. elephant's	elephant (25)	baby
	baby elephant (6)	
	elephant baby (87)	
will have	have (46)	go (2)
	got to go (2)	want to go
	got (16)	won't have (2)
	have to (3)	got to have
	you'll have (3)	you wanta
	gonna have to (4)	gonna
	gonna hafta go	got have
	gotta go	gotta
	gonna have (5)	would have
12. is		feels (2)
		feel (4)
		was (2)
feels	feel (113)	make
		fill
13. had	didn't have no (101)	wouldn't have
	have no	no (3)
	got no	won't got
	ain't got no (2)	wouldn't ha' no
	ain't had no	
	didn't have any (11)	
	don't got no	
	have	
	hadn't got no	
	don't have no	
	didn't ha'	
shoes	shoe (11)	she
14. is	Mary's absent (8)	was (65)
	Mary's	I
	(deletion) (7)	ain't
	didn't go to school	
was	is (22)	thought hen's sick

No. Word	*Reconstructions*	*Errors*
	she's sick (10)	think's so
		she's (2)
15. boys	boy (32)	girls
		man
		mothers
		ladies
		baby
lots	a lot (48)	all the milk
	lot (9)	some
	a lots (7)	(distortion)
		of lot
		gettin'
16. things	thing (57)	anything (4)
		something
		lots
friends	friend (99)	people
		in the lunch room
17. has	got (11)	had (5)
	gonna have	will have (6)
	have (56)	might be
	ha' (28)	(distortion)
	have to be	ought
	gots (2)	better
		better be
		should be
		will be
		was asked (2)
		should
have	get (3)	will not have him
	ha' (2)	has (3)
	gets	won't have no (2)
		do nothing
		(distortion) (3)
		wouldn't getta go
		go

No.	Word	Reconstructions	Errors
			wouldn't get nothing
			be (6)
			give
			won't
			do (3)
			don't do
18.	stairs	stair (35)	
		steps (7)	
		step	
	talked	talk (58)	had to talk to
		talkin' (2)	was tending
		was talking (12)	kicked him
		was talk (4)	caught
		been talkin'	he talk
		was talked	tookin
		was talkin' (45)	was walkin'
			drop
19.	will give	give (16)	had to give
			will
			(distortion)
			will let you
			will have you give
			a smile
			have give (3)
			wants to give
			have
			ha' give
			will was
	you have	you finished (84)	teacher finished
	finished	you are finished (2)	you do (3)
		you finished (13)	(distortion)
		you get finished (6)	you will finish
		you'll finish	you have doing
			he has finished
			she's finish
			you hadin

No. Word	*Reconstructions*	*Errors*
20. papers	paper (48)	'tations
	paper work	teacher (2)
		work
will be	be (33)	will give (2)
	would be (2)	will (4)
	will get	might be
	teacher'll be (3)	teacher'll give
		you a smile
		are
		would know
		would
21. she's	she (30)	her got
	she has (19)	she had (2)
	she got (50)	teacher (2)
	she has got (2)	she gonna (3)
	she gots (5)	she give
	she have (2)	I got
she's	she (26)	(distortion)
	she going (17)	I'm going
	she'll (2)	
	she give (2)	
	she gonna (9)	
	she goin'	
	she will give (2)	
	she'll give me	
	she is going (5)	
	she'll give	
	she gives	
	she will (6)	
I'm	I be (61)	I was
	I am (2)	she nice (2)
	I (4)	I'm gonna to give be
		you be (2)
		I'll nice
22. if	did (128)	to
		what

No. Word	Reconstructions	Errors
		is (2)
		does
		when (2)
said	say (39)	se
		told me
23. are	(deletion) (11)	do (4)
		was
		have
		is
		ha'
you've eaten	you eat (60)	you
	you have eating	we eat
	you're eaten	you have
	you finish eaten	you are eating
	eaten (2)	you finish (3)
	you get finish eatin'	I eat
	gettin' eaten	you are eaten (2)
	you eating	you get eating
	you've aten	eating
	you finish eating (2)	
	you eaten (75)	
	you finished	
	eaten (2)	
	you have eaten (6)	
24. ate	eat	came
		has aten
25. felt	feel (5)	came (2)
	fell (15)	feels
	feelin'	was sick (3)
		has
		got
		was (12)
came	went (2)	couldn't come
	he did come	didn't come
	come (3)	he's going
		couldn't go

No. Word	*Reconstructions*	*Errors*
26. is not	ain't (8) isn't (2) don't make	not (5) make (3) is (20) don't (2) (distortion) (3) can't
makes	make (31) is (49) are	it's was isn't
27. will give	give (14) gonna give	will have given (2) gave (2) has given (2) will will given was gonna will get

He has eaten	he's ha' eaten (2)
	he been eatin'
	he had eaten
	he have aten (2)
	he get finished
	he has ate
	he finished eating
	he gets finished
	   eating
	he had eaten (2)
	he has aten (2)
	he finished eaten (3)
	he's finish aten (2)
	he has finished
	   eating
	he has finished
	he finishes
	   eating (2)
	he ate (4)
		he have
		had he eaten
		he was eating

No. Word	*Reconstructions*	*Errors*
	he eat (26)	
	he have eaten (6)	
	he finish eating	
	he's ate	
	he ha' aten	
	he was eaten	
	he gets finish his	
	he would eaten (2)	
	he eatin'	
	he aten (3)	
	he has had eaten	
	he's eaten (4)	
	he has eat	
	he's finished (3)	
	he eats (13)	
	he finishes (6)	
	he finish (7)	
	he eaten (25)	
	he's eat	
	he does eaten	
	him eaten	
28. is not	ain't (13)	is
	isn't	not (16)
	ain't not	nots
		are not

Unique Reconstructions
Rural Blacks
(N = 54)

1. was tied		tied
2. isn't a	ain't a	is not (3)
	is not a	(distortion)
		is (2)
		is a
		was a

No. Word	Reconstructions	Errors
3. wants	want (8)	
4. movies	movie (15)	
5. said	say (2)	
toys		
6. did	was	does
		(distortion)
mother	mama	
7. was caught	got caught (3)	(distortion)
		then caught
		was cracked
		had been caught
beaten up	gotten beaten up (2)	tied up
	gotten beat up	
	beat up (6)	
	got beat up	
	beatened up (2)	
8. I'm not going to	I won't get any (7)	I didn't get
	I won't get (2)	
	I don't get	
	I ain't gonna (5)	
	I won't (8)	
	I'm not gonna (7)	
	not gonna get	
	I'll not get	
	I won't get none	
	I not gonna	
	I not get any	
	I'm not (omit) get any (2)	
	I wouldn't get any	
	I don't get none	
9. was hit	got hit (7)	is hit
		hit (2)
		was trying to hit

No.	Word	Reconstructions	Errors
	jumped	was jumping rope (5)	is jump
		jump (3)	by the jump that was hit in the street
		was jumping (3)	was jump
		was jump roping	that
		jump rope (2)	
10.	runs	run (17)	went (3)
			hurry
			ran (2)
			walked
			rides
	has	got (6)	had (10)
		he's got	ha'
		have (6)	
		he got (3)	
11.	elephant's	elephant baby (22)	another baby
		baby elephant (2)	
	will have	have (20)	won't have
		gonna have (2)	
		got (3)	
		must have	
		you'll have	
12.	is		
	feels	feel (24)	has
13.	had	didn't have no (24)	
		don't have no (5)	
		didn't have any	
		don't got no	
		hadn't got	
	shoes	shoe	have
14.	is	Mary's (3)	was (9)
			(distortion) (2)
	was	is (4)	want
		she's sick	she's
			was
			(distortion)

No.	*Word*	*Reconstructions*	*Errors*
15.	boys	boy (12)	
	lots	a lot (11)	(distortion)
16.	things	thing (14)	something
	friends	friend (21)	(distortion)
			boy
17.	has	got (5)	had
		will have	
		ha' (3)	
		have (2)	
	have	got	has
		ha' (2)	won't be
18.	stairs	stair (8)	street
		steps (2)	
	talked	was talking (5)	was
		was talkin' (9)	
		talk	
19.	will give	give (2)	will smile
		give you (2)	
	you have	you finish (15)	
	finished	you did	he finish
		you done (2)	
		you would finish	
		finish (2)	
		you	
20.	papers	paper (21)	
	will be	be (8)	
		would be	
21.	she's	she gots	she is going
		she got (13)	
		she has (4)	
	she's	she is going (3)	
		she is goin'	
		she is	

No.	Word	Reconstructions	Errors
		she will give (2)	
		she give	
		she'll	
		she will	
		she gonna (2)	
	I'm	I be (18)	I will be
		I am	
22.	if	did (19)	
	said	say	
23.	are		do you do (2)
			have
			did
	you've eaten	you're done	I eat
		you eating	you're eating
		you eat (10)	was eaten
		you eaten (12)	
		you have eaten (4)	
		you finish eating	
		when you get	
		through	
		you done aten	
		eaten	
24.	ate	eat	
25.	felt	feel (2)	was (3)
			because
			when
	came	come (7)	went
26.	is not	don't make	(distortion) (2)
		is ain't	makes
		ain't	not
		is not make	is about
			is (4)
			would not
			don't
	makes	make (7)	don't make
		is (7)	it is

No. Word	*Reconstructions*	*Errors*
	would make	
	are	
27. will give	give (3)	he aten
	mother'll give	
he has eaten	he ate (3)	him eat
	he eats (4)	is not eaten up
	he aten (2)	aten
	he has ate (2)	
	he eat (2)	
	he has aten (3)	
	he would eat	
	he gets through eating (2)	
	he's eaten	
	he through	
	he has finished eat'n	
	he have	
	he eatin' (2)	
	he have eaten (2)	
	he finishes	
	he have aten	
	him eaten	
	he eatens	
	he's ate	
28. is not	ain't (6)	(distortion)

Unique Reconstructions
Rural Whites
(N = 211)

1. was tied		is tied (2)
		tied
2. isn't a	ain't (2)	is a (4)
	isn't no (4)	is (12)
	is not	was (2)
	ain't a (2)	(distortion) (3)
	isn't not a	wasn't

No. Word	Reconstructions	Errors
3. wants	want (9)	
4. movies	movie (10)	hisself
5. said		dere's
toys	toy (6)	
6. did	was (7)	
mother	mama (4)	she
	mothers	(distortion)
7. was caught	got caught (11)	was (4)
	was being	was tried (3)
	caught (2)	was tryin'
	was crushed	was tied up
	was crashed (2)	caught (2)
	was questioned	was quiet
	was caughten	was stopped
		tried to
		was (distorted)
		them caught
		was
		was in an accident
beaten up	got beaten up (12)	ate
	beat up (14)	was tied up
	get beat up (3)	to tied up
	beated up (2)	beaten
	beatened up (4)	got all et up
	was beaten	
	was beaten up	
8. I'm not	I'm not gonna (37)	I never got any
going to	I don't (12)	(distortion)
	I ain't get	I didn't get
	I ain't gettin any (2)	I can't
	I ain't gonna (38)	they won't get none
	but I bet I'm not	but then I didn't
	gonna get any	get any
	I won't get none	I don't want
	I will not	he ain't getting

No. Word	Reconstructions	Errors
	I not gonna	I won't (3)
	I won't even get	I'm going to wait til
	none	I didn't wanna go
	I don't think I'll get	get any
	I don't get any (3)	I don't bet I will
	I'm not getting (3)	get any
	I ain't getting	
	I won't get any	
	I don't get	
	I'm not get any	
	I better not bring	
	any (2)	
	I'm not gonna get	
	ice cream	
	I know I won't get	
	I'm no' gonna get	
	I won't get (4)	
	I won't gonna	
9. was hit	got hit (20)	hit
	was hitten	was hitting
		was
		was runned over
		was jumped
jumped	was jumpin' (2)	was jumping in the
	jump (9)	street
	jumping rope	(omit rope) (2)
	who was jumping	be hit
	rope	jumping (2)
	jump roping	was in the road
	was jumping rope	was jumped (2)
	(11)	who was in the road
	was jumpin' rope	was jumping in the
	(4)	road
	jumps rope	
	jump rope (3)	
	was jumping (11)	

No. Word	*Reconstructions*	*Errors*
	jumpin' rope	
	was throwin' the	
	rope in the street	
10. runs	run (29)	went (4)
		runned (3)
		ran (4)
		rides (3)
		rans
has	have (4)	he can ride
	had (11)	on his bike
	he's got (5)	
	got	
	he got (2)	
11. elephant's	elephant baby (13)	had
	baby elephant (14)	a baby
	another baby	elea's baby
		elephant (2)
		baby's elephant
		baby (5)
will have	have (74)	you go to the
	will go	will you have
	you (delete have)	ought
	(3)	want
	you'll have (5)	
	you'd have (2)	
	you have (4)	
	would have (3)	
	got (2)	
	you gotta go	
12. is		feel
		feels (2)
feels	feel (29)	like (2)
		wants to (3)
		feeling
13. had	didn't have no (109)	had

No. Word	*Reconstructions*	*Errors*
	didn't have any (6)	wouldn't didn't
	never had no (3)	wear no (2)
	did not have no (2)	wouldn't have no
	has	(2)
	don't have no (3)	
14. is	Mary's	was (71)
	Mary's absent	was father
	her teacher let her	mother thought he's
	be absent	sick
		(distortion)
was	she's sick (10)	so she's sick
	is (18)	mother is (2)
		thinks
		her's
		think her sick
		mother's sick
15. boys	boy (21)	girls (2)
	boy was gett'n	
lots	a lot (74)	box of
	much (2)	notes
	gived a lots	more
	alot lunch	(distortion)
	a bunch	too much (3)
	lot	
	whole bunch	
	a lote (7)	
16. things	thing (28)	anything (4)
		anythings
		(distortion)
friends	friend (60)	
	girl friends	
	neighbors	
17. has	got's	won't
	has got	have quietly

No.	Word	Reconstructions	Errors
		got (2)	should
		needs	better be
		have to (2)	or else his teacher
		haf to (2)	wouldn't
		have (13)	
		must	
		ha' (5)	
	have	get (9)	no
			won't get
			give
			give him
			do (2)
			he wants (2)
			ha'
			go on
			go out to play
			go out at
			go outside for recess
			or else his teacher
			wouldn't
18.	stairs	steps (7)	
		stair (2)	
	talked	was talkin' (104)	was watchin' (5)
		talk (6)	was tending
		mama's talking	was talked
		mother's talkin'	babies
			he's talkin' (2)
			he had
			tendin'
			was holding
			watched
			was feeding
			was watching (3)
19.	will give	give	you'll give (2)
	you have	you ... finish (17)	you're

No. Word	Reconstructions	Errors
	you (47)	teacher
	you get finished (2)	get you through
	you finish (44)	have you
	you are through	
	you do all of	
	you would finish	
	you're finished	
	you get (3)	
	you're all finished	
finished	finish (22)	"f"
		doin your work
		get through
		through (3)
20. papers	paper (51)	pages
		if you do your work
will be	be (14)	will
		would be
		is
21. she's	she got's (4)	she will give (2)
	she got (21)	this girl
	she has got (9)	her
	(reversed order	she will (3)
	scored correct)	I've got
	she has (14)	
	she gonna	
	she have	
she's	she going (4)	she will give me a
	she'll (5)	happy
	she gonna (4)	that girl is going
	she give (2)	
	she will give (7)	
	she'll give (4)	
I'm	I be (64)	will
	I (6)	(distortion)
	I am (8)	he's be

No. Word	*Reconstructions*	*Errors*
	I'll be	I was (3)
		she will give me a
		lollipop
		she's
		he is (3)
22. if	did (62)	would
said	"sa—"	except
23. are	(delete are)	will you be
	be doin'	have (2)
		eating
		do you do (2)
		did (4)
		is
		will
		do
		(distortion) (3)
you've eaten	you have eat	you ate
	you eat (74)	you gonna do
	you eaten (36)	eating
	you finished	
	get through eaten	
	you get through	
	eating (3)	
	you have aten	
	you already eat	
	you get done	
	eating (3)	
	you have eaten (6)	
	you're eating (2)	
	you had eaten	
	you eating	
	you was eating	
	you are eating (3)	
	you get through	
24. ate	eat (26)	
25. felt	feels	was (5)

No.	Word	Reconstructions	Errors
		feeled	but
		come	when
		feel (8)	is
		thought he was	was sick
		seemed	got (2)
		feeling	
	came	come (73)	went (4)
		got (2)	go
26.	is not	ain't (12)	is (8)
		don't mean	makes
		don't make (2)	I don't
		not makes	
		isn't (3)	
		doesn't make	
		doesn't	
	makes	make (7)	is ain't
		will make	
		is (70)	
		equals	
27.	will give	you'll give	gives (2)
		he eaten	(distortion) (5)
		give (2)	will cook
	he has eaten	he eats (4)	he hadn't eaten
		he's has eaten	
		he eat (5)	
		he eats (67)	
		he gets through eating (3)	
		he get through eating	
		he gets eating	
		he has aten (4)	
		he ate (3)	
		he gets done eating (2)	
		he is eating	

No. Word	*Reconstructions*	*Errors*
	he finish	
	he has had	
	he's aten	
	he's ate (2)	
	he has finished	
	he's through eaten	
	he's eat	
	he gets finished eaten	
	he gets finished	
	he's eaten (16)	
	he's finished	
	he got through eatin'	
28. is not	ain't (40)	that animal is dead,
	isn't (2)	not dead
	wasn't	have not
	ain't not	
	is ain't	

Unique Reconstructions
Inner-city Puerto Rican
(N = 124)

1. was tied		is tied
		uh tie
2. isn't a	ain't a (6)	(distortion) (2)
	is not a	is a (2)
		is (4)
		wasn't a
		uh
		isn't
3. wants	want	(distortion)
4. movies	movie (50)	
5. said	say (21)	
	Say	
	says (3)	
toys	toy (20)	Jamie's
		boys

No. Word	*Reconstructions*	*Errors*
6. did		is there
		(distortion) (4)
		she sa
		is
		would
		what
mother		you
		(distortion)
7. was caught	got caught (4)	got
	been caught	then caught
	was caught up	was (2)
		den caught
		caught
		they caught
		(distortion)
		was trying to
		to be caught
beaten up	beat up (9)	beat him up (2)
	got beat up (5)	was eaten up
	got beaten up (7)	caught up
	beating up	was beated up
	was beaten	
	was beating up (2)	
8. I'm not	I'm not gonna (31)	(distortion) (6)
going to	I won't (13)	I'm gonna
	I'm never gonna	I won't want any
	I not gonna (9)	I'm gonna get any
	I ain't gonna (15)	I know better
	I won't get any (4)	I wasn't gonna
	I'm never going to	I am gonna
	I won't get (3)	I can't
	I'm not to get any	I don't want to get
	I ain't gonna have	I cannot get any
	I'm not getting	I gonna get any
	I don't	
	I am not gonna	

No. Word	Reconstructions	Errors
	I'm not getting	
9. was hit	got hit (17)	hit (8)
	got hurt	was by hit
		what hit
		boy's hit
		who hit
		was bit
		were hitten
jumped	was jumping rope (17)	was jump (3) (distortion)
	jump (23)	jumping (6)
	jumping rope	jumps (2)
	was jumping jump rope (2)	was jumped
	was playing jump rope (4)	
	jump roping	
	playing jump rope	
	was jumping by the street	
	was jumping (8)	
	was jumping on the street (2)	
	was jump roping	
	was jumpin' right on the street	
	was jumping in the street (3)	
	was playin' jump rope (2)	
	jumping rope	
	was jump ropin'	
10. runs	run (32)	rides (2)
		went
		goes (2)
		ran (13)

No. Word	Reconstructions	Errors
		comes
		go
		gets
has	got (14)	had (14)
	gots (14)	runs
	have (4)	run
	owns	
	ha' (2)	
11. elephant's	elephant (5)	animal baby
	elephant baby (39)	is
	baby elephant (5)	baby's elephant (4)
	baby (2)	
will have	gotta go (2)	(distortion)
	have (66)	gonna
	got (4)	will want
	gotta	will go
	will has	want
	gonna have (2)	are gonna have
	you'll have	
	you have	
12. is		feels (3)
		looks
		was
feels	feel (47)	(distortion)
	feeling (4)	looks
13. had	didn't have no (70)	(distortion) (3)
	don't have no (8)	got no
	don't got no (4)	won't have no
	have no	has
	didn't have any (7)	hadn't
	don't have any (2)	didn't get no
	ain't have any	
	ain't got no	
	didn't have	
	doesn't have no	
	didn't have (4)	

No. Word	Reconstructions	Errors
	doesn't have any	
	didn't got	
	didn't got no	
	didn't gots no	
	doesn't got	
	don't have any	
	doesn't have	
	don't got	
shoes	shoe (6)	(distortion)
		(skoose?)
14. is	(deletion) (2)	was (52)
was	is (8)	she's
15. boys	boy (3)	(distortion)
		mothers
		girls
		girl
		lady
lots	alot (64)	glass of
	alots	many
	whole bunch	some
	lot (2)	
16. things	thing (29)	(distortion) (2)
		some
		something
		anything (2)
friends	friend (81)	boys
17. has	have (14)	got (3)
	must (2)	should have
	gots (2)	would have (2)
	is supposed to be	must have
	must be	is supposed
	ha' (6)	better be
		should
		better behave
		will have (2)
		was asked

No. Word	Reconstructions	Errors
have	get (13)	(distortion) (3)
		has
		be (2)
		give (3)
		go
		won't give
		give him
		go out to
		should not
		do (3)
		so
		don't have no
		would let him
18. stairs	stair (12)	
	stairways	
	steps (5)	
	step (3)	
talked	talking	was taking care of
	was talking (35)	was taking care
	talk (34)	was trying
	is talking	was holding (2)
	was talkin'	feel on the baby
	talks (3)	took
	was talking to	(distortion)
		taught
		held
		fell down the baby
		ha'
		took care
		was hitting
		spoke
		was toting
		was looking
		came down
		was quiet
		went to get

No. Word	Reconstructions	Errors
		was holdin'
19. will give	give (3)	gonna get
	gonna give	will smile
you have	you (91)	you will
	your work is finished	you don't (2)
		(distortion)
		you are (2)
finished	finish (100)	answer
		do (4)
		give
20. papers	paper (36)	(distortion) (2)
	paper work	meal
will be	be (6)	(distortion) (2)
	would be	are
	will get	will (3)
		will smile
		might be
21. she's	her got (2)	he got
	she gots (25)	you got
	she has (33)	she had
	she got (16)	she gave
	she have (2)	
	she has got	
	the teacher got	
she's	she give (4)	she might give
	she will give (16)	she was gonna
	she gives	she will going
	she gonna give (3)	she will gonna
	she'll give	
	she going (13)	
	she gonna (4)	
	she is going (2)	
	she will	
	she might give	
	she is gonna	
	she's giving me	

No. Word	Reconstructions	Errors
	she'll give	
	she'll	
I'm	I be (39)	I will be
	I (6)	(distortion)
	be	you be
	I gonna	I behave
	I was	
	I am (2)	
22. if	did (9)	in
		that
		is (3)
		what (2)
		to
		(distortion)
said	say (12)	(distortion)
	told me	tell me
	says	
23. are	(deletion) (7)	(distortion) (2)
		do you do (4)
		do
you've eaten	you eat (46)	you're eating (14)
	you finish (5)	(distortion) (5)
	you eaten	eating (3)
	you have eaten	you doing eating
	you have to eaten	you have to eat
	you eaten (10)	you have
	you eating (16)	you leave
	ya eaten	he eat
	you have finished	you got
	you've eating (2)	you are eaten
	you have eating	
24. ate	had ate	(distortion)
	eat (4)	didn't eat
	eats	
	et	
25. felt	was (27)	got (3)

No. Word	Reconstructions	Errors
	feel (3)	became
	fell (9)	fall
	was feelin'	came sick
		tel?
came	went (25)	couldn't go
	come (5)	didn't go
	ca'	didn't come (3)
	doesn't make (5)	equals (2)
26. is not	ain't (9)	(distortion)
	does not make	was
	doesn't equal	is (4)
		are not (2)
		not (2)
		makes
		will make
makes	is (41)	
	make (11)	
	are (3)	
	equals (2)	
27. will give	is gonna give (2)	will get
	gonna give	will have given
	give (6)	
	's gonna	
he has eaten	he finishes (12)	(distortion) (2)
	he eat (7)	you're finish
	he has ate (2)	he gives
	he eats (36)	you eat
	he's finished with	he was eating
	he finish eating (2)	he is eats
	he eating (2)	he got
	he ate (4)	she's eat
	he finished (2)	to eat supper
	he's eating (2)	
	he eaten (7)	
	he finish (6)	
	he's eaten	

No. Word	Reconstructions	Errors
	he have eaten	
	he has eat up	
	he finishes eating	
	he ha finish	
	he has finish	
	he has eating (3)	
	he has finished (3)	
	he has eat	
28. is not	ain't (16)	is
	was not	no have
	isn't	not (3)

We feel these data have demonstrated our major assertion: Many lower-class children speak a dialect which is different from the language of the school. These children are not language delayed but may be in need of intensive language experiences to enable them to master the language of the school. In addition, some lower-class children are at a normal level of language development, but are reluctant to use language in formal settings. For these children, enrichment activities presented through games and experiences described in Chapter 8 will assist them in making the transition from the low demands for language in the home to the high demands for language competency in the school.

SUMMARY

1. Lower socioeconomic children of various ethnic groups (white, black, Puerto Rican) will change a sentence to conform to their own (home) dialect.
2. These changes or reconstructions are correct forms of the child's dialect.
3. Children who omit words rather than reconstruct words tend to be slower developmentally and have more difficulty with reading.
4. Lower-socioeconomic white children are more delayed in acquiring some forms than inner-city blacks or Puerto Rican

children. Thus, rural poverty may not provide the experiences necessary for these children to develop some language forms.

5. The Anastasiow/Hanes SRT can be used to individually diagnose a child's level of language usage and assist teachers in planning their daily classroom program.

In the next chapter, we will discuss function words and general cognitive functioning.

CHAPTER 7   FUNCTION WORDS

New forms are first used to express old content while new
content is first expressed in old forms.
                    PIAGET, 1955; SLOBIN, 1973

OUR THESIS THROUGHOUT the chapters has been that the poverty
child acquires language in a similar manner as that employed by the advantaged child. Until now our discussions have
relied on the basic principles of language acquisition and the
general processes by which the child, advantaged or disadvantaged, constructs his knowledge of the world. We have attempted to point out that there are universals in language acquisition
which are based on the nature of cognitive processing and the
nature of language in general. We have now reached the point
at which specific explanations of our language data in relation
to developmental differences and similarities among subcultural
groups will more fully emphasize our thesis.

Our original problem of developing a means of assessing language development which would not be influenced by dialectal
differences led to an examination of classes of words which are
not typically altered in dialectal translation. Simply stated, if
dialectal differences can be identified by the way the lower-class child pronounces words and how he structures his sentences
("I ain't got none."), are these differences also found in the
child's understanding of the meaning or definition of words?

While our studies could have focused on sentence structure or
the use of nouns, verbs, prepositions, or pronouns, we have
chosen a more general approach in order to gain knowledge
about a child's general level of language development. Therefore, our interest has been in the acquisition of words that serve
an important use in language but are more abstract than nouns;
these are called function words.

Neisser (1967) has identified two general categories of words

111

used in language: content words and function words. As we pointed out in Chapter 2, the content words category generally includes nouns, pronouns, and verbs. These words relay a specific amount of information. For example, the word *boy* has a specific object referrent which can be defined as having certain attributes. Similarly, the word *jump,* another content word, has a specific action referrent. That is, the word alone conveys a notion with definable attributes. In contrast, function words convey a meaning in reference to a particular sentence. Most function words have no meaning by themselves; they must have other words in order to convey meaning. Compare the content word *horse* with the function word *who.* The word *horse* immediately conveys information, whereas *who* must have a logical sentence for it to make sense. As another example, the word *because* conveys or indicates a causal relationship between or among two acts; however, the full definition of a particular causal relationship is dependent on the sentence in which *because* is located. In other words, function words derive their full meaning from the sentence in which they appear. Therefore, function words can be ambiguous when removed from the context of a linguistic expression. Consider the ambiguous response a four-year-old child might give to the question, "Why did you do that?": "Because." The response does not specify anything other than the implication that there was, indeed, a reason for the action. Similarly, the removal of function words from a sentence adds to the ambiguity of the sentence or the meaning to be conveyed. An example of this would be as follows:

(a) The boy hit the red ball.
(b) Boy hit ball.

In brief, function words are ambiguous when they are not expressed in some specific context. Somewhat conversely, sentences are more ambiguous when function words are not included.

From our brief review, the reader should recognize the importance of function words in language development. In the process by which the child becomes a competent user of language, function words obviously present a dual problem for the child. The problem, although similar to that faced in acquiring all words, is even more complex, since the use of function words requires a knowledge of how these abstract things *(who)* or events *(then)* can be represented in sentences, as well as the appropriate word for representing a particular event. Take as an example the sentence:

1. John and Mary are happy.

In understanding or producing the sentence, the child must have knowledge of three factors: (a) the fact that two events—(1) John is happy and (2) Mary is happy—can be represented in a combined manner; (b) that representing two equivalent events in a sentence involved coordination of the subjects and modification of the verb; as well as, (c) that *and* is the appropriate symbol to use in the coordinated expression. This example may be too simplistic to convey the complexity of the process; however, elaboration on our example may more clearly demonstrate the point.

Prior to the child's ability to say "John and Mary are happy," the child may express the same intention in the form:

2. John is happy and Mary is happy.

Obviously, the production of sentence 2 is less complex than that of sentence 1, since the child does not have to change either of the basic structures expressed in the two separate components —(1) John is happy, and (2) Mary is happy. The significance of the three types of knowledge discussed earlier is represented in the sentence:

3. John is happy but Mary is sad.

The young child of four or five years may produce or reproduce sentence 3 in the form:

4. John is happy and Mary is sad.

To produce sentence 4 in the form of sentence 1 requires several modifications or transformations. Piaget (1971) and others have noted the inappropriate use of *and* in spontaneous speech samples similar to sentence 4. Our analysis of sentence 4, in relation to the three types of knowledge required in using function words would suggest: (1) that the child may have the knowledge that two adverse events may exist within a unit of space or time; (2) that the child may not have the knowledge of how to express those events as being coordinated and yet adverse; or (3) that the child does not have the knowledge of the appropriate symbol to express the adversity of the events.

At this point the significance of the interaction of cognitive processing and grammatical complexity discussed in Chapters 2 and 3 should be more apparent. Perhaps this interaction is best expressed in a set of interdependent relationships. First, the use of the appropriate function word is dependent on an understanding of an event or state ("John is happy"—the child must understand happy) and on a knowledge of function words. Second, an understanding of how to use words appropriately is dependent on a knowledge of how language is organized in a particular culture and the appropriate word to represent thoughts or ideas. Third, an understanding of language is dependent on the child's ability to delete and substitute words and forms.

In summarizing the differences between content and function words, the major distinction is that function words obtain their meaning and use primarily in respect to language. The abstract quality of the operations required in the appropriate use of function words provides the rationale for our selecting function words as one measure in assessing general language development.

Therefore, the language which a child understands is closely related, theoretically, to the language which he can produce. We found in our earlier studies that function words are acquired by children later in their language acquisition than content words. Many function words *(while, although)* are mastered some time after six years of age.

We suspected that words which represent very abstract concepts would not be acquired by *all* children, whether they resided in poverty or not, until around eleven or twelve years of age, the time when Piaget suggests most children can reason in terms of abstractions.

We included function words in our Sentence Repetition Task primarily to demonstrate that both middle- and lower-class children would have difficulty with these words. If both groups had difficulty, then we could argue that the poverty child's lack of acquisition of function words was a normal developmental stage and not due to economic or genetic problems. As stated in an earlier chapter, this assumption was the basis in the development of a task which could be used as a general measure of language development in the classroom.

For our purposes the following function words were constructed into the sentences developed for our sentence repetition measure:

1. —
2. —
3. Where . . . what
4. Then
5. Whose (retention of interrogative)
6. Did (retention of interrogative) . . . while
7. who . . . then
8. although
9. by the girl (retention of passive marker) . . . who
10. after school (retention of temporal) . . . because
11. If . . . then
12. when
13. wouldn't (retention of negative) . . . because
14. because
15. by the ladies (retention of passive marker)
16. either . . . or; not (retention of negative conditional)
17. or
18. while
19. when
20. If . . . then; neater . . . happier (retention of comparative)
21. which . . . if
22. if . . . didn't (retention of negative)
23. what . . . after
24. couldn't (retention of negative) . . . because

25. Although
26. because
27. When
28. because

Function words are

scored correct if:
   1. Repetition is verbatim.
   2. Response is stated twice, once correct, the other time wrong.
   3. In sentence 8, *although* bears similarity to *ah-toe*.

scored as substitutions and correct if:
   1. Function word substitution retains full meaning of the sentence.
   2. In sentence 13, *wouldn't* is substituted by *didn't* or *doesn't*.
   3. In sentence 16, *or not* is substituted by *or don't* or *say nothing*.
   4. In sentence 20, *neater* and *happier* are substituted by *cleaner* and *nicer*.
   5. In sentence 22, *didn't* is substituted by *not* or a similar negative.
   6. In sentences 9 and 15, there is retention of the passive structure requiring use of *by* regardless of the noun in the phrase.
   7. In sentence 10, *after school, after* is substituted by another temporal preposition (for example, *before school*).

scored as errors if:
   1. Response given is incorrect according to the Key and not a valid substitution.
   2. Words are distorted beyond intelligibility. This happens if the response simply cannot be understood, even though it is evident that a sound was made in the correct "response slot."

Two scores were obtained regarding function words: function word omissions, and function words correct. We predicted that function word omissions would be an indication of developmental delay. When a child repeated a sentence by omitting the word, we assumed that the logical construction is beyond the child. For example, we found most first through fourth graders would omit the *then* in the sentence, "If you want to see an elephant, then you'll have to go to the zoo." The *then* can be omitted and the resulting sentence makes sense by simple association.

While the theoretical bases suggested that the sentence repetition technique should be a valid and reliable measure of language, our initial studies were focused on empirically establishing the reliability and validity of the instrument (we were able to establish a test—re-test reliability of r = .74).

In a pilot study of inner-city, black, poverty children, random samples were drawn from each grade level including kindergarten through grade six. Analyses of the number of function words correct indicated a significant increase across each grade level. Similarly, the number of function words omitted decreased significantly across each grade. These results suggested that the specific scoring procedures of focusing on function words did reflect the developmental changes that were expected as language acquisition progressed. In brief, the results of this initial study suggested that significant developmental changes in the function word class may be a valid measure of general language development, as well as the fact that the sentence repetition technique is a highly reliable procedure.

An additional study of normal and mental-retardate children was conducted to examine the influence of experience and mental growth on the use of function words (Anastasiow & Stayrook, 1973). As was predicted, the performance of mental retardates closely resembled that of their mental-age peers. This suggested that the developmental changes that were observed in the pilot study described above may have been primarily a function of intellectual development. This conclusion was supported by the theoretical position that cognitive development is a necessary condition for language development; however, the data from this study was only suggestive of that conclusion.

In order to more carefully examine the relationship between language and cognitive development, a third study was conducted with black inner-city and white rural-poverty children, as well as with a sample of white middle-class children. Each child in the study was administered the sentence repetition task and a Piagetian seriation, discrimination, and numeration task. The samples were drawn from three grade levels: kindergarten, first grade, and second grade. Scores from the Piagetian task were intercorrelated with function word scores in order to examine the relationship between our general measure of language development and cognitive development. While Piagetian task scores correlated positively with the number of function words correct, the strongest relationship was found in a negative correlation between Piagetian task scores and the number of function words omitted. These results suggested that cognitive functioning was critically related to the child's knowledge of relationships expressed by different function word classes; whereas, knowledge of specific function words (function words correct) may be more closely related to the child's general knowledge of the language.

Since the poverty samples performed less well than the middle-class sample on both measures, we were also interested in determining whether differences in cognitive development could account for the differences in language performance. An analysis of covariance was performed in order to test this hypothesis (Anastasiow & Hanes, 1974). In essence, the analytical procedure adjusted and equalized differences in cognitive development in order to determine if differences in language development still existed. The results of this procedure indicated that black inner-city poverty children performed equivalent to middle-class children on the sentence repetition task when differences in cognitive development were equalized.

In general, this third study substantiated the relationship between language and thought suggested by the earlier investigations. It also supported our belief that the poverty child performs linguistically much like his middle-class peer when differences in cognitive development are taken into consideration.

A fourth study investigated the amount of heterogeneity in language development among three distinctly different groups of poverty children. The following table shows the developmental similarity of omissions among racial groups:

Grade	Blacks	N	Whites	N	Puerto Ricans	N
1	6.9	(100)	10.4	(104)	11.0	(47)
2	5.4	(92)	7.6	(121)	8.7	(35)
3	5.6	(26)	5.9	(94)	7.0	(36)

Our experience with different groups of children convinced us that environmental differences within one socioeconomic status level do influence language development. In our fourth study, large samples were drawn from two eastern, inner-city areas and a southern, rural area. The inner-city samples included bilingual, Puerto Rican and black, poverty children. The rural sample was almost exclusively white, poverty children. Our analysis indicated that the black children performed better than the other two groups, and the Puerto Rican children performed better than the white rural group. The implication in the data was that the isolation related to living in a southern rural area was perhaps more detrimental to language development than the situation faced by the bilingual inner-city child. A second year follow-up of a selected sample from all three groups strengthened this explanation. Again the black children performed better than the other two groups, and the Puerto Rican children performed better than the white sample.

In the following pages we have presented the number of children who omit, substitute, or make errors on function words. Note that the tendency is for children to make a great many omissions on words that represent more abstract aspects of thought, such as "who," "then," "either," "which," and "because." Also note the similarities across subcultural groups on particular items. This last point clearly suggests to us that the children in each of the groups are acquiring language in a similar manner and sequence.

Function Words

Rural Appalachia

Word	No.	Blacks (N = 48)			Whites (N = 212)		
		Errors	Omis.	Subs.	Errors	Omis.	Subs.
where	3	3	4	0	28	16	0
what		8	3	0	15	12	0
then	4	0	5	0	2	19	0
whose	5	0	2	21	1	2	19

Word	No.	Errors	Omis.	Subs.	Errors	Omis.	Subs.
did	6	2	3	1	0	11	6
while		0	5	18	6	25	94
who	7	2	30	0	0	126	4
then		0	40	1	3	171	1
although	8	9	16	6	46	62	5
by the girl	9	1	6	3	4	30	15
who		0	13	8	3	70	89
after school	10	8	15	0	36	89	0
because		1	13	0	2	57	0
if	11	2	3	0	2	24	0
then		0	33	0	0	189	0
when	12	0	3	0	3	6	6
wouldn't	13	1	1	5	0	4	22
because		0	2	0	3	16	1
because	14	4	10	0	1	49	3
by the ladies	15	13	11	6	67	63	20
either	16	3	46	0	0	223	3
or not		7	13	9	9	53	56
or	17	3	8	3	5	33	19
while	18	0	1	6	10	9	24
when	19	2	2	6	1	9	22
if	20	1	4	5	27	21	4
then		0	39	0	3	179	0
neater		4	3	1	15	26	7
happier		14	4	1	31	19	1
which	21	0	39	9	7	188	16
if		0	11	3	4	36	1
if	22	0	12	21	1	67	61
didn't		1	5	1	3	24	3
what	23	1	3	0	0	7	0
after		0	4	9	3	16	51
couldn't	24	0	0	1	4	3	5
because		1	2	0	16	12	1
although	25	5	16	0	5	69	1
because	26	2	26	0	5	123	1
when	27	1	1	5	9	3	77
because	28	2	6	0	2	26	0

Function Words

Inner-City

Word	No.	Blacks (N = 230)			Puerto Ricans (N = 124)		
		Errors	Omis.	Subs.	Errors	Omis.	Subs.
where	3	6	4	0	14	4	0
what		29	2	1	17	7	0
then	4	4	4	0	3	7	0
whose	5	0	1	53	36	4	1
did	6	2	15	4	8	15	0
while		4	10	62	5	12	75
who	7	1	49	6	3	55	6
then		3	58	0	1	83	0

Word	No.	Errors	Omis.	Subs.	Errors	Omis.	Subs.
although	8	31	35	2	21	41	1
by the girl	9	14	23	12	9	22	10
who		9	73	34	3	41	19
after school	10	37	85	0	35	64	0
because		3	30	0	6	42	0
if	11	8	36	0	2	13	3
then		2	143	0	1	92	0
when	12	4	12	4	5	3	1
wouldn't	13	8	5	35	2	5	44
because		5	16	0	5	14	0
because	14	3	23	0	4	19	0
by the ladies	15	62	53	2	39	32	17
either	16	16	132	0	7	105	0
or		16	25	8	2	23	10
not		16	40	57	2	28	55
or	17	10	26	40	3	18	29
while	18	12	9	35	14	13	30
when	19	17	7	23	15	2	8
if	20	4	26	28	23	11	12
then		20	143	34	1	92	26
neater		19	25	1	6	13	6
happier		75	22	1	43	9	1
which	21	3	148	17	4	88	22
if		4	33	10	9	36	10
if	22	5	22	127	18	21	0
didn't		1	5	1	3	9	5
what	23	4	8	0	1	11	0
after		5	9	18	13	17	32
couldn't	24	0	4	7	1	2	10
because		2	3	0	3	6	1
although	25	42	45	9	21	39	4
because	26	3	49	0	2	76	1
when	27	3	9	62	8	9	35
because	28	3	23	0	5	14	0

One particularly interesting response young children make is the substitution of *when* for *while,* for example in the sentence, "Did the accident happen while your mother was in the store shopping?" *When* implies a definite time, whereas *while* implies duration.

It would appear to us, from our studies, that children who reside in poverty make every attempt to respond but do so by *utilizing their own language patterns.*

In the pages that follow, note the variety of ways children repeat sentences. As with reconstructions, some responses we call correct because they are consistent with lower socioeconomic dialects. Some forms we have labeled as errors due to the fact that they are not consistent with the syntax of most forms of English as it is accepted in the schools.

Function Words

Rural Blacks

(N = 47)

No. Word	Substitutions	Errors
1. —	—	—
2. —	—	—
3. where		what (3)
what		where (3)
		whats
		(distortion)
		when (3)
4. then		
5. whose	who (21)	
6. did	was	does
		(distortion)
while	when (18)	
7. who		(distortion)
		when
then		and
8. although	but (5)	I bet (2)
	and though	all there
		and then
		but I bet (4)
		but I'm
9. by the girl	by the boy (2)	(distortion)
	by a boy	
who	that (8)	
10. after school		from school (5)
		from
		at the school
		for school
because		

No.	Word	Substitutions	Errors
11.	if		
	then		has then
12.	when		
13.	wouldn't	would not (4)	(distortion)
		didn't	
		won't (2)	
	because		
14.	because		I think
			when
			(distortion) (2)
15.	by the ladies	by all the lunchroom	in the ladies (3)
		by the girls	(distortion) (3)
		by the lady (3)	from the ladies (3)
			to the lady
			when the lady
			of
			to
16.	either		(distortion)
			(even? or ever?)
	or not	or say anything (2)	then
		or nothing (2)	not
		nothing	or all
		don't say	either
		or don't	or anything (2)
			but
			you can't say
			nothing
17.	or	'cause (2)	(distortion)
		because	an
			that
18.	while	when (6)	
19.	when	if	(distortion) (2)
		after (3)	
		while (2)	
20.	if	when (5)	that
	then		

No. Word	Substitutions	Errors
neater	neatier	neat (3)
		(distortion)
happier		happy (14)
21. which	what (3)	
	that (6)	
if	when (3)	
22. if	did he (2)	
	did (19)	
didn't	hasn't	wouldn't
23. what		when
after	once	
	when (8)	
24. couldn't	didn't	
because		
25. although		al . . .
		because
		oh (2)
		(distortion)
26. because		but (2)
27. when	after (12)	before
	if (3)	
28. because		but
		when

Function Words
Rural Whites
(N = 211)

1. —	—	—
2. —	—	—
3. where		why
		what (16)
		when (2)
		be (3)
		(distortion) (5)
what		when (7)

No. Word	*Substitutions*	*Errors*
		(distortion) (2)
		we're (4)
		why (2)
4. then		(distortion)
		when
5. whose	who (19)	what
6. did	was (6)	
while	when (93)	(distortion) (4)
	whenever	why (2)
7. who	that (4)	
then	but	caught
		tried
		but him
8. although	though (2)	but I bet (12)
	and though (3)	all boy
		but I know (3)
		all I want (9)
		how 'bout
		but I ain't
		you know
		(distortion)
		if (6)
		but (7)
		while
		oh! do
		then
		that though
9. by the girl	by a jump rope (3)	the girl
	by the boy (3)	with the girl
	by a rope (2)	when
	by a girl	while the girl
	by a boy	
	by the rope (3)	
who	what (37)	when (2)
	that (42)	(distortion)

No. *Word*	*Substitutions*	*Errors*
10. after school		to school (9)
		at school
		from school (19)
		in from school
		at home
		to home
		from
		to the school (2)
		to his school
because		and
		when
11. if		'cause
then		
12. when	whenever (4)	like (2)
	if (2)	'cause
13. wouldn't	will not (3)	
	don't want him to	
	didn't (11)	
	won't (3)	
	would not (4)	
because		
14. because	'cause	(distortion)
		when (2)
15. by the ladies	by a lady	from the ladies (25)
	by the lady (7)	from (3)
	by the boys	from the lady
	by the girls (5)	to the ladies (11)
	by the woman's	to the boys
	by the woman (3)	from the girls (5)
	by the women	when the ladies
	by women's in the	for the girl
	milk	because of the ladies
		because the ladies
		(3)
		to the women's

No. Word	Substitutions	Errors
		from the women (2)
		with the lady
		in the restroom
		cause the lady
		the ladies are getting milk
		from the lady in the restroom
		in the ladies' lunchroom
		for the ladies (3)
		to the lady in the bathroom
		lunch ladies in the milk because
		with the people
16. either		always (2)
		(distortion)
or not	or nothing (4)	if don't say (2)
	or don't (14)	and
	or say anything (2)	either (2)
	don't (11)	need
	or not anything	anything (3)
	none	
	nothin' (13)	
	or say nothing (4)	
	but (2)	
	say nothing (4)	
	don't say	
	don't say anything	
	or should not say anything	
17. or	'cause (13)	(distortion) (3)

No. Word	Substitutions	Errors
	because (3)	so
	for (3)	unless
18. while	when (24)	'cause (5)
		because (2)
		(distortion)
		whenever
		why
19. when	after (11)	(distortion)
	if (4)	
	once	
	while (5)	
	whenever	
20. if	when (27)	'cause
then		good
		happier (2)
neater	cleaner	neat (12)
	neatier (6)	nice
		good
		nice and clean
happier	gladier	happy (29)
		help you
		proud of you
21. which	that (14)	when
	what (2)	if
		and (2)
		'cause
		(distortion)
		and she's gonna
if	when	(distortion) (3)
		cause
22. if	did he (3)	would
	did (58)	
didn't	did not	wouldn't (2)
	no	(distortion)
	he said no	

No. Word	Substitutions	Errors
23. what		
after	when (50)	while (2)
	whenever	if
24. couldn't	can't	have no (2)
	didn't get to	after tomorrow
	didn't (2)	(when)
	wouldn't	can't
because	'cause he come	when (3)
		but
		Jimmy felt sick
		when he went to
		school
25. although	but (2)	also
		oh (3)
		on account of
		(distortion)
		always
		well
		all (7)
		ah so
26. because	on account of	but (5)
27. when	after (73)	if (9)
	whenever (3)	while (2)
	when	
28. because	on account of	but

Function Words
Inner-city Black
(N = 210)

1. —	—	—
2. —	—	—
3. where		what (2)
		when (5)
		can

No. Word	Substitutions	Errors
		which
what	as	if
		when (21)
		where (5)
		which
		who
		want
4. then		en
		daddy
		now
		though
		these (3)
5. whose	who (71)	
6. did	was there	there
	was it an accident	is (2)
	was (2)	when (8)
while	when (77)	to (2)
		did
		en
		with
7. who	that (6)	what
then		but
		and
		and tried
8. although	though	an though
		also (12)
		all boy
		I bet
		almost
		ah (2)
		of course
		why
		and then (2)
		ah so
		all (7)
		and

No. Word	*Substitutions*	*Errors*
		well
		oh (2)
		oh oh
		but (4)
9. by the girl	by a jump rope (2)	the girl
	by a car	while the girl
	by a rope (5)	(distortion)
	by the rope (2)	by jumpin'
	by the boy (2)	but the boy
		when the girl (8)
		was girl
who	that (34)	(distortion)
		was
		what (2)
		with (2)
		when (3)
10. after school		from school (23)
		(distortion)
		from (3)
		a school
		by the school
		when he get to school
		at school
		at home (2)
		to school (4)
because		but (3)
11. if		do (7)
		is
then		
12. when	while (2)	like (3)
	if (2)	where
13. wouldn't	didn't (23)	let him
	won't (5)	
	couldn't	
	can't (2)	

No. Word	Substitutions	Errors
	did not	
	would not (2)	
	don't	
because		(distortion) (4)
		but
14. because		but
		was
		and
15. by the ladies	by the lunchroom (2)	from the ladies (17)
		for the boys
		in the lady
		when the ladies (5)
		in the ladies (7)
		for the ladies (3)
		to the ladies (3)
		with the ladies (3)
		while the ladies (4)
		while the lady
		but
		for the lady
		cause the lady
		was the ladies
		with the lady
		of the lady (2)
		from the lady (9)
		when the boys
16. either		even (10)
		neither (3)
		really
		never
		at least
or		but (8)
		and (2)
		(distortion)
		on either (2)

No. Word	Substitutions	Errors
		on don't (9)
		if
		I cause
not	don't (18)	anything at all
	no things at all	anything (2)
	say nothing (23)	say anything (12)
	say no	say it
	say nofhin'	or either at all
	nothing (5)	neither
	either say nothing at all	neither say neat
	or either nothing	or say
	don't say (2)	
	you don't say nothing at all	
	you say nothing at all	
	shouldn't say anything (2)	
	even nothing	
	shouldn't	
	either say nothing	
17. or	cause (22)	so (4)
	else (10)	unless (3)
	because (4)	but (2)
	for (2)	before
	less (2)	
18. while	when (25)	who (2)
		cause (2)
		steps
		before when
		an
		and
19. when	if (4)	'cause (2)
	after (13)	(distortion)
	before	is

No.	Word	Substitutions	Errors
		while (5)	and
			one
			in
20.	if	when (28)	en'
			is (3)
			in
	then		yet
	neater	cleaner	finished
		neatier (3)	neat (14)
			be here
			nice
			finish
			greater
			later
	happier	nicer	happy (56)
			like them (17)
			hap
			what's happenin'
21.	which	that (12)	if
		what (5)	that if
	if	when (8)	'cause
			(distortion)
			s' I
			as
			is (2)
22.	if	did (127)	to
			what
			when (2)
			is
	didn't	did not	did
23.	what		when (2)
			where
			for when
	after	when (18)	unless
			while (4)
24.	couldn't	didn't (2)	

No. Word	Substitutions	Errors
	shouldn't	
	can't (3)	
	doesn't	
because		(distortion)
		but
25. although	but (9)	all
		thought
		all then
		I say
		when
		'ole
		oh (6)
		all (12)
		oh oh (3)
		ah so
		all boy
		all bet
		ah
		I know
		also (9)
		all but
26. because		but (3)
27. when	if (15)	as (2)
	after (47)	is
28. because		but (2)
		or

Function Words
Puerto Rican

(N = 124)

1. –	–	–
2. –	–	–
3. where		what (3)
		were (3)
		when (5)

No. Word	Substitutions	Errors
		(distortion)
		why
		woo
what		where (5)
		were
		when (9)
		(distortion) (2)
4. then		now
		well
		(distortion)
5. whose	who (36)	when
6. did		is there
		would
		what
		(distortion) (3)
		(she sa . . .)
		is
while	when (75)	(distortion) (3)
		that
		after
7. who	that (6)	when
		(distortion)
then		the one was
		but
8. although	though	(distortion) (2)
		oh boy!
		oh (2)
		all (2)
		when
		I always
		all bet
		all no
		bet . . . but
		if
		ah so
		I bet

No. Word	Substitutions	Errors
		oh my
		all then
		boy!
		all better
		ah no
		I oh
9. by the girl	by a jump rope	with the girl (3)
	by a girl (3)	on the girl
	by the rope	to school
	by a boy	in the girl (2)
	by the boy (2)	into the girl
	by a rope	in the
	by the dog	
who	that (19)	when
		when she
		though
10. after school		to school (17)
		from school (15)
		for school
		in the school
		from the school
because		but (2)
		(distortion)
		before
		when (2)
11. if	when (2)	is
		in
then		well
12. when	if (3)	(distortion)
	(distorted if)	where
13. wouldn't	won't (8)	no
	didn't (24)	(distortion)
	don't (5)	
	no like	
	doesn't (3)	
	not	

No. Word	Substitutions	Errors
	no want	
	couldn't	(distortion) (2)
because		but (3)
		(distortion)
14. because		while
		maybe
		if
15. by the ladies	by the lady (10)	on the ladies
	by the lunchroom (4)	(distortion) (2)
		to the lady
	by his mother	from the ladies
	by the women	with the ladies (2)
		from the lady (9)
		from the lunchroom
		from
		in the ladies (3)
		of the lady (2)
		because the lady (4)
		when the lady (2)
		from the lunch
		boys-girls-lady
		to the ladies
		because
		even
		neither
		of
16. either		even (4)
		and (3)
or		but (6)
		then
		nut
not	don't (10)	anything at all
	nothing (23)	
	no	

No. *Word*	*Substitutions*	*Errors*
	should not say anything	
	say nothing (15)	
	none	
	do not	
	shouldn't	
	nothing to your friends at all	
	not anything	
17. or	because (9)	but (2)
	'cause (14)	before (2)
	or else (6)	and
18. while	when (30)	because (2)
		(distortion) (3)
		cause
		until
		by
		why
		but (2)
		before
		with
		if
19. when	after (5)	(distortion) (5)
	if (6)	because
	while (3)	before
	once	until
20. if	when (23)	
then		(distortion)
neater	nicer	(deliter?)
	nicier	neat
	neatier (2)	neatly
	neatest	good
		(distortion)
		clean
happier	happiest	happy (37)

No. Word	*Substitutions*	*Errors*
		laugh
		smile (3)
		hap
		neater
21. which	that (20)	if (3)
	what (2)	(distortion)
if	when (8)	(distortion) (3)
		why
		see
		to be (2)
		but is
22. if		did (8)
		in (2)
		is (3)
		what (2)
		that
		to
		(distortion)
didn't	no (3)	(distortion)
	don't	couldn't
	no (2)	done did it
23. what		(distortion)
after	when (32)	(distortion) (4)
		before (3)
		if (2)
		at
		while (3)
24. couldn't	didn't (7)	(distortion)
	not	
	would not	
	didn't have no	
because	for	but (2)
		while
25. although	even though (2)	(distortion) (2)
	though	all (7)
		and all

No. Word	Substitutions	Errors
		also (3)
		ahso
		wonder when
		oh (2)
		all so
		as
26. because	for	while
		but
27. when	after (22)	(distortion) (6)
	before	as (2)
	as soon as	
	if (11)	
28. because		but (2)
		while
		(distortion)
		he goes

SUMMARY

Our findings with function words are very similar to those with reconstruction words with the addition that:

1. Children who omit a large number of function words have more difficulty with reading.
2. Children from all socioeconomic levels omit function words of more abstract forms (e.g. if-then, either-or, while, who).

Implications:

1. Children acquire the form, pronunciation, and syntax of the language of their home.
2. Children can understand the language spoken at school and do so by repeating sentences correctly by translating them into the language of their home.
3. Children learn language through direct experiences; if children are to learn the language of the school, direct experiences must be provided in school for the child to make this transition.

The remainder of the book will be addressed to this last issue.

CHAPTER 8 TEACHING CHILDREN FROM LOWER SOCIOECONOMIC GROUPS

"Listen to them, talk to them."
GEORGIA COOPER

WE HAVE NOTED that all too often children who reside in different cultural subgroups frequently reside in poverty. Not only are the experiences of these children different from those of white middle-class children, but also their language differs in predictable ways from the language of the school.

The language these children speak is a normal outgrowth of their past experiences and learnings. To us, their thinking ability or intelligence can be defined or described only in terms of the cultural context in which they live and have been reared. All social classes contain some children who are developmentally delayed, but our data suggest that the mass of lower-class children we have studied possess normal intellectual functioning and language development. From our point of view, their difficulties with reading are cultural and are in the main due to the school's failure to modify initial reading and language instruction to match the past experiences of the child and to provide *direct, concrete* experiences with school English.

An analysis of programs developed to enhance the language development of poverty children indicates that three basic approaches predominate in these programs: (1) informal emphasis on language expression, (2) modeling techniques, (3) expansion and extension techniques. Informal emphasis on language is reflected in the teacher's encouragement of language usage in all classroom and outdoor activities with no specific lessons in language, e.g. Weikart's Cognitively Oriented Curriculum. Model-

142

ing techniques are based on the assumption that children learn language by imitating the language in their environment. In a modeling situation the teacher constructs a linguistic sequence, e.g. a sentence, and requests that children model or repeat verbatim the original sequence, e.g. DISTAR Language Program. The technique of expansion depends on an informal emphasis on language since the teacher utilizes the language produced by the child as the basis of her response. That is, the teacher expands the language produced by the child to include new words and new constructions. In expanding the child's language the teacher does not call attention to the child's errors. The teacher attempts to extend the child's knowledge of language by progressively expanding his language to include new words and new constructions.

The results of a number of programs indicate that each approach to language instruction can be effective in influencing development. More importantly, programs utilizing more than one approach to language instruction have demonstrated the most gains in development (Moore, 1971). Therefore, our concern is not with the specific approaches that a teacher selects for instructions; our concern is that multiple approaches are offered based on the characteristics of the children. The Sentence Repetition Task was designed in order to provide the teacher with a means of determining the language characteristics of the children in his/her class.

As a result of the research reported in previous chapters, we have concluded that the Sentence Repetition Task differentiates four categories of children. Since each category relates to a specific combination of scores on the Task, the teacher can make some inferences for the types of instructional activities that might be most appropriate for each group of children.

In general the results of our studies indicate that the Sentence Repetition Task does identify four distinctly different groups:

1. children who consistently use a nonstandard vernacular and are delayed in language development;
2. children who consistently use a nonstandard vernacular but are at a normal level of language development;

3. children who may be delayed in language development and use a standard vernacular;
4. children who use a standard vernacular and are at a normal level of language development.

BILINGUAL CHILDREN

While our major concern has been with the dialect-speaking child of poverty, we have encountered a number of situations involving language instruction for the bilingual child. The task of learning the language of the school is similar for the dialect-speaking child and the non-English speaking child even though the non-English speaking child is faced with learning a language distinctly different from the language of his home. Our experience with English language instruction for Spanish-speaking children is generally consistent with the position that many bilingual educators have taken (*see* Asher, 1972). We have two suggestions: (1) Delay the teaching of reading until the child has mastered English, or preferably, (2) teach the child to read in Spanish and after third or fourth grade switch to English. We feel that the personnel at the Southwest Regional Educational Development Laboratory (211 East 7th Street, Austin, Texas 78701) have had great success with their bilingual language program, and the interested reader should contact them or a specialist in bilingualism for further suggestions.

Alfredo Castaneda (1974) has provided an excellent overview of the needs of the Mexican-American child. Castaneda points out that the Mexican-American child is socialized to the group or the family rather than self-oriented. Any achievement or failure the child experiences is perceived as a reflection on the family. The notion of family is a broad one which includes family relatives, but also close neighborhood or community members. The child, Castaneda states, is taught to respect the total "family" and demonstrate appropriate social behaviors in their presence. Thus, school tasks, if not perceived by the child as part of enhancing the family's reputation or goals, may not be perceived as important to the Mexican-American child.

Castaneda suggests that the curriculum for the Mexican-American child must be humanized and personalized. Castaneda also recommends the use of humor, fantasy, cooperative group work and high adult-pupil contact. Castaneda provides extensive teaching suggestions which should be extremely useful for teachers who teach a Mexican-American child.

It should be kept clearly in mind that any description of a group, such as Mexican-American, is a group description. There are vast individual differences in all groups. These descriptions of groups should be used as a guide for teacher planning, not as absolutes.

LANGUAGE AND READING

It has been well documented that the child's language development is related to his ability to learn how to read. Too often we have assumed the level of a child's language from his oral speech. By now the reader should realize oral speech is a small sample of a poverty child's language and may be a very inadequate reflection of the child's competence.

In learning how to read English, one of the major tasks is for the child to recognize that written words represent or are symbols for sounds. Thus, the letters *M I L K* read *milk* to the child who previously has learned the name *milk* and knows what the English word *milk* stands for. One of us has discussed the relation between oral language and reading at length elsewhere (Anastasiow, 1971). Our position is that the cultural variables in the poverty child's ability to learn to read are his intelligence, his ability to comprehend language as it is spoken in school, and the teacher's acceptance of the child's dialect.

In the current studies with the Hampton Institute Nongraded Follow Through Model, we find that Function Word Omission scores are negatively related to reading test scores in the first through fourth grade. Thus, Function Word Omission scores can be used to predict which children will have difficulty with reading due to slower intellectual or language development. However, total number Reconstruction Words Correct are positively related to reading test scores. This is a particularly important point, since it indicates the children who speak a dialect of poverty can succeed on regular school tasks such as reading school English.

Our studies also indicate that, given a program of ungraded curriculum, children who reside in poverty make significant gains year by year. The set of data provided below are typical of our larger sets of findings. At grade one the children were reading at the 44 percentile, grade two, the 48 percentile, and by grade three, the 57 percentile. Thus, when children are allowed to proceed at their own pace, in an atmosphere where dialect is allowed and enriched language experiences are provided, there appears to be a steady increase in children's reading ability.

We firmly believe that when direct experiences are provided for the learning of school English through such activities as word games, rhythmic activities, experiences with toys and puppets, children who speak different dialects can succeed in mastering school English. For some children the process is rapid and can be achieved in kindergarten (or preschool). For others, it may be necessary to allow a year or two for the child to become knowledgeable of school English.

Remedial lessons which focus on deficits appear to us to be inappropriate strategies to deal with these children. We have found lessons that deal with the child's strengths to be very successful.

And what are the child's strengths? We believe them to be the following:

Most poverty children possess a language that is as well developed as that of other children their age. (Low Function Word Omissions)

Implications:

(1) Allow the child to use his language but provide him with many models of school English.

(2) Allow time for child-to-child communication.

(3) Allow and plan for a variety of experiences with objects, textures, places, people, media.

(4) Encourage the child to talk about his experiences.

(5) Model language; don't correct the child when he is communicating with you.

(6) Plan lessons that cover common deficits. For example, if a child has not experienced a pear, bring in a pear to eat,

smell, feel, accept, reject. Bring in pictures and/or toys following a direct experience, rarely before.

Children's language is an integral part of the self.
   Implications:
   (1) Accept children's language as it is and provide models for the desired form. Attacks on a child's language are attacks on the child.
   (2) Provide praise and reinforcement of desirable children's language and ignore forms and words that are considered unacceptable.
   (3) Encourage and praise communication efforts.

Children learn to express how they feel in terms of their emotions and are in general overwhelmed and frightened in unfamiliar settings.
   Implications:
   (1) Familiarize children with you as the teacher. Discuss with children your expectations and what school is like.
   (2) Ask children what they like and listen to them.
   (3) Watch for nonverbal communication signs of children's feelings. If children show marked confusion, ask yourself what is it you are communicating nonverbally.
   (4) Try to avoid any assumptions about children's past experiences; what may be a toy and therefore a reward to you may be perceived by the child as something you do in school and therefore a school task, not a reward. We found in one poverty setting that children felt doing puzzles was school work and not play, contrary to our expectations.

Vary the cultural setting of the school activity to the culture of the child.
   PAST, PRESENT AND FUTURE TENSE

A fundamental rule of development we have stressed throughout the book is that knowledge precedes performance. Knowledge is acquired through the child's direct experience. Therefore, we recommend that teachers do not assume that a child has experienced an event unless the teacher has observed that the child has had such an experience.

In the Durham Education Improvement Project, two gifted teachers (Mrs. Alma Bennett and Cora Peaks) had great success with the following game:

Children are seated in a small group.

Teacher: Alpha, please go and open (present tense) the door. (note the teacher does not imply a choice—avoid "would you like to")

Alpha gets up, walks across the room and opens the door.

Teacher: Class, what did Alpha do?

Class: She opened (past tense) the door?

Teacher: Yes, Alpha walked over and opened the door. Now Alpha, close the door.

Alpha closes the door.

Teacher: Class, what did Alpha do?

Class: Alpha closed the door.

Teacher: Alpha, you may sit down. Who will (future tense) open door next? (Hands raised) Sandra and Robert, go and open the door.

Sandra and Robert open the door.

Pronouns

Teacher: What did they do?

Class: They opened the door.

The lessons can be varied to include opening, shutting and sitting, standing, and so on. Note that "ing" endings are frequently absent in poverty dialects and these direct experiences will introduce them.

Concepts such as "on top of," "inside of," "beside of," "underneath" can all be directly experienced with a large table. The lessons have several advantages: (1) children experience them, (2) other children observe them, (3) all children hear and produce the standard form, (4) success is easily obtained, and (5) children enjoy them.

In addition, plurals and past tense "ed" forms frequently united in the speech of the poverty child can be encouraged through play.

DICTATED STORY

Many teachers have found that children's written expression can be developed by encouraging a child to dictate his own story to a picture he has painted or experience he has had. At first many of these stories are simple and contain incomplete sentences. Accept the child's product and print or type it for him. Later read it back to him and see if he feels it says enough. Our experience has been that many children will wish to expand upon their story. In an atmosphere of support and encouragement, children's stories become more complex. Successful techniques with older children are to have them write stories in response to music, tape recorded city sounds or magazine pictures.

CHART STORIES

Taking time to have the class (or small group) review their direct experience (field trip, game) by dictating a summary or story about it is a useful language stimulation technique. Stories can be written on the board or on chart paper. Teachers have found that other children will assist slower developing children in selecting the appropriate tense or word form.

SUMMARY

Any number of techniques which encourage language expression will enable you to assess children's language development.

For the child who omits words on the Sentence Repetition Task, time, encouragement and frequent experiences will do much to encourage development. Motor activities, rhymthic involvement, and verbalization of activities are desirable strategies.

For the child who tends to reconstruct school English, experiences with school English will greatly assist his ability to read school English. He may or may not reduce his oral dialect—in fact, we find many children do not reduce their reconstructions until they are beyond sixth grade.

Many children who reside in poverty can succeed in school and do. For most of the children who do not, we believe it is the failure of the school to begin instruction where the child is when he enters school and to accept the child as a normal functioning human being who needs experiences his environment has not provided if he is to succeed in school.

RECOMMENDED READING

Landeck, B.: *Learn to Read, Read to Learn.* New York, David McKay Co., 1975.

BIBLIOGRAPHY

Anastasi, A.: *Differential Psychology*, 3rd ed. New York, Macmillan, 1958a.

Anastasi, A.: Heredity, environment, and the question "how?" *Psychological Review*, 65:197, 1958b.

Anastasiow, N. J.: Success in school and boys' sex-role patterns. *Child Development*, 36:1053, 1965a.

Anastasiow, N. J.: Progress Report: Evaluation of the Story Reading Program. (Mimeo) Palo Alto, California, 1965b.

Anastasiow, N. J.: *Oral Language: Expression of Thought*. Newark, International Reading Association, 1971.

Anastasiow, N. J.: Educating the culturally different children. *Viewpoints*, 48(2):21, 1972.

Anastasiow, N. J., and Hanes, M. L.: Language reconstructions as an indicator of cognitive functioning of k-third graders. Indiana University, Bloomington, Institute for Child Study, 1974a.

Anastasiow, N. J., and Hanes, M. L.: Sentence repetition task. Indiana University, Bloomington, Institute for Child Study, 1974b.

Anastasiow, N. J., and Stayrook, N. G.: Miscue language patterns of mildly retarded and nonretarded students. *American Journal of Mental Deficiency*, 77(4):431, 1973.

Anastasiow, N. J., Stedman, D. J., and Spaulding, R. L.: Language and reading among disadvantaged nursery and primary grade children. *The Slow Child*, 17(1):39, 1970.

Anderson, S. A., and Beh, W.: The reorganization of verbal memory in childhood. *Journal of Verbal Learning and Verbal Behavior*, 7:1049, 1968.

Anglin, J. M.: *The Growth of Word Meaning*. Cambridge, M.I.T. Press, 1970.

Asher, J.: Children's first language as a model for second language learning. *Modern Language Journal*, 55:133, 1972.

Bandura, A.: *Principles of Behavior Modification*. New York, Holt, Rinehart and Winston, 1969.

Bandura, A., and Walters, R. H.: *Adolescent Aggression*. New York, Ronald Press, 1959.

Baratz, J. C.: Teaching reading in an urban Negro school system. In Baratz, J. C., and Shuy, R. (Eds.): *Teaching Black Children to Read*. Washington, Center for Applied Linguistics, 1969.

Baratz, J. C.: Relationship of black English to reading: A review of research. In Laffey, J. L., and Shuy, R. (Eds.): *Language Differences: Do They Interfere?* Newark, International Reading Association, 1973.

Baratz, J., and Shuy, R.: *Teaching Black Children to Read.* Washington, Center for Applied Linguistics, 1969.

Bartlett, F. C.: *Remembering.* Cambridge, Cambridge University Press, 1932.

Bee, H. L., Van Egeren, L. F., Strissguth, A. P., Nyman, B. A., and Leckie, M. S.: Social class differences in maternal teaching strategies and speech patterns. *Developmental Psychology, 1:*726, 1969.

Bellugi, U., and Brown, R. (Eds.): The acquisition of language. *Monograph of the Society for Research in Child Development, 29*(92): 1964.

Bereiter, C., and Engelmann, S.: *Teaching Disadvantaged Children in the Preschool.* Englewood Cliffs, Prentice Hall, 1966.

Berko, J.: The child's learning of English morphology. *Word, 14:*150, 1958.

Berlyne, D. E.: *Structure in Directions in Thinking.* New York, Wiley, 1965.

Bernstein, B. B.: A critique of the concept of compensatory education. In Cazden, C. B., John, V. P., and Hymes, D. (Eds.): *Functions of Language in the Classsoom.* New York, Teachers College Press, 1972.

Bever, T. G.: The cognitive basis for linguistic structures. In Hayes, J. R. (Ed.): *Cognition and the Development of Language.* New York, Wiley, 1970.

Birch, H. G., and Gussow, J. D.: *Disadvantaged Children: Health, Nutrition and School Failure.* New York, Harcourt, Brace and World, 1970.

Bower, G. H., Clark, M., Winzenz, D. J., and Losgold, A.: Hierarchical retrieval schemes in recall of categorized word lists. *Journal of Verbal Learning and Verbal Behavior, 8:*323, 1969.

Bowlby, J.: Separation anxiety. *International Journal of Psycho-Analysis, 41:*80, 1960.

Braine, M. D. S.: The ontogeny of English phrase structure: The first phase. *Language, 39:*1, 1963.

Brown, R.: *A First Language: The Early Stages.* Cambridge, Harvard University Press, 1973.

Brown, R., and Fraser, C.: The acquisition of syntax. In Cober, C. N., and Musgrave, B. S. (Eds.): *Verbal Behavior and Learning: Problems and Processes.* New York, McGraw-Hill, 1963.

Butterfield, E. C., and Cairns, G. F.: Discussion summary—infant reception research. In Schiefelbusch, R. L., and Lloyd, L. L. (Eds.): *Language Perspectives: Acquisition, Retardation, and Intervention.* Baltimore, University Park Press, 1974.

Butterfield, E. C., and Zigler, E.: The effects of success and failure on the discrimination learning of normal and retarded children. *Journal of Abnormal Psychology, 70:*25, 1965.

Castaneda, A.: The educational needs of Mexican-Americans. In Castaneda, A., James, R. L., and Robbins, W.: *The Educational Needs of Minority Groups.* Lincoln, Professional Educators Publications, 1974, pp. 13-43.

Castaneda, Carlos: *Journey to Ixtlan.* New York, Simon and Schuster, 1972.

Caudill, W., and Schooler, C.: Child behavior and child rearing in Japan and the United States: An interim report. *Journal of Nervous and Mental Disease, 157*:323, 1973.

Cazden, C. B.: *Child Language and Education.* New York, Holt, Rinehart, and Winston, 1972.

Cazden, C. B.: Play with language and metalinguistic awareness: One dimension of language experience. *International Journal of Early Childhood, 6*(1):12, 1974.

Cazden, C. B., John, V. P., and Hymes, D.: *Functions of Language in the Classroom.* New York, Teachers College Press, 1972.

Chilman, C. S.: *Growing Up Poor.* Washington, U.S. Department of Health, Education, and Welfare, 1966.

Chomsky, N.: *Aspects of the Theory of Syntax.* Cambridge, M.I.T. Press, 1965.

Chomsky, N.: *Cartesian Linguistics.* New York, Harper & Row, 1966.

Chomsky, N.: *Language and Mind.* New York, Harcourt, Brace and Jovanovich, 1972.

Chomsky, N., and Halle, M.: *The Sound Pattern of English.* New York, Harper & Row, 1968.

Coles, R.: *Migrants, Sharecroppers and Mountaineers.* Vol. 2 of *Children of Crises.* Boston, Little, Brown and Co., 1972.

Coles, R.: *The South Goes North.* Vol. 3 of *Children of Crises.* Boston, Little, Brown and Co., 1973.

Condon, W. S., and Sander, L. W.: Synchrony demonstrated between movements of the neonate and adult speech. *Child Development, 45*: 456, 1974a.

Condon, W. S., and Sander, L. W.: Neonate movement is synchronized with adult speech: Interactional participation and language acquisition. *Science, 183*:99, 1974b.

Cronbach, L. J.: *Essentials of Psychological Testing.* New York, Harper & Row, 1970.

Davis, A.: Socio-economic influences upon children's learning. *Understanding the Child, 20*:10, 1951.

Deutsch, C.: Auditory discrimination and learning: Social factors. *Merrill Palmer Quarterly, 10*:277, 1964.

Deutsch, M.: The role of social class in language development and cognition. *American Journal of Orthopsychiatry, 35*:78, 1965.

Deutsch, M., and Associates: *The Disadvantaged Child.* New York, Basic Books, 1967.

Eimas, P. D., Siqueland, E. R., Jusczyk, P., and Vigorito, J.: Speech perception in infants. *Science, 171*:303, 1971.

Ervin, S. M.: Imitation and structural change in children's language. In Lenneberg, E. H. (Ed.): *New Directions in the Study of Language.* Cambridge, M.I.T. Press, 1964.

Ferguson, C. A., and Slobin, D. I. (Eds.): *Studies of Child Language Development.* New York, Holt, Rinehart and Winston, 1973.

Flavell, J. H.: *The Developmental Psychology of Jean Piaget.* New York, Van Nostrand Reinhold, 1963.

Fodor, J., and Garrett, M.: Some reflections on competence and performance. In Lyons, J., and Wales, R. J. (Eds.): *Psycholinguistic Papers.* Edinburgh, University of Edinburgh, 1966.

Fraser, C., Bellugi, V., and Brown, R.: Control of grammar in imitation, comprehension, and production. *Journal of Verbal Learning and Verbal Behavior, 2*:121, 1963.

Frasure, N. E., and Entwisle, D. R.: Semantic and syntactic development in children. *Developmental Psychology, 9*(2):236, 1973.

Furth, H. G.: Research with the deaf: Implications for language and cognition. *Psychological Bulletin, 62*:145, 1964.

Furth, H. G.: Concerning Piaget's view on thinking and symbol formation. *Child Development, 38*:819, 1967.

Ginsburg, H.: *The Myth of the Deprived Child.* Englewood Cliffs, Prentice Hall, 1972.

Goslin, D. A. (Ed.): *Handbook of Socialization Theory and Research.* Chicago, Rand McNally, 1971.

Gray, S., and Klaus, R. A.: An experimental preschool program for culturally deprived children. *Child Development, 36*:887, 1965.

Guskin, J.: *The Social Perception of Language Variation: Black and White Teachers' Attitudes Toward Speech from Different Racial and Social Class Background.* Ann Arbor, University Microfilms, 1970.

Heinicke, C. M.: Some effects of separating two-year-old children from their parents. *Human Relations, 9*:106, 1956.

Hess, R. D., and Shipman, V.: Early experience and the socialization of cognitive modes in children. *Child Development, 36*:869, 1965.

Hobson, J. R.: Scholastic standing and activity participation of under-age high school pupils originally admitted to kindergarten on the basis of physical and psychological examinations. *News Letter,* Division of School Psychologists, APA, 1956.

Hollingshead, A. B.: *Two Factor Index of Social Position.* Cambridge, Yale University, 1965.

Horner, V. M., and Gussow, J. D.: John and Mary: A pilot study in linguistic ecology. In Cazden, C. B., John, V. P., and Hymes, D. (Eds.): *Functions of Language in the Classroom.* New York, Teachers College Press, 1972.

Huey, E. B.: *The Psychology and Pedagogy of Reading.* Cambridge, M.I.T. Press, 1968.

Hunt, J.: *Experience and Intelligence.* New York, Ronald Press, 1961.

Inhelder, B., Bovet, M., Sinclair, H., and Smock, C. D.: On cognitive development. *American Psychologist, 21:*160, 1966.

Jacobson, R.: *Child Language, Aphasia and Phonological Universals.* The Hague, Mouton, 1968.

Jensen, A. R.: How much can we boost IQ and scholastic achievement? *Harvard Review, 39:*1, 1969.

Kagan, J.: On the need for relativism. *American Psychologist, 22:*131, 1967.

Karnes, M. B., Teska, J. A., Hodgins, A. S., and Badger, E.: Educational intervention at home by mothers of disadvantaged infants. *Child Development, 41:*925, 1970.

Kohlberg, L.: The concepts of developmental psychology as the central guide to education: Examples from cognitive, moral, and psychological education. In Reynolds, M. C. (Ed.): *Proceedings of the Conference on Psychology and the Process of Schooling in the Next Decade: Alternative Conceptions.* Minneapolis, University of Minnesota, 1971.

Labov, W.: The logic of nonstandard English. In Williams, F. (Ed.): *Language and Poverty.* Chicago, Markham, 1971.

Labov, W.: *Language in the Inner City: Studies in the Black English Vernacular.* Philadelphia, University Pennsylvania Press, 1972.

Lakoff, G.: Linguistics and natural logic. In *Studies in Generative Semantics.* Ann Arbor, University of Michigan, Phonetics Laboratory, 1970.

Langacker, R. W.: *Language and Its Structure.* New York, Harcourt, Brace and World, 1968.

Lenneberg, E.: *The Biological Foundation of Language.* New York, Wiley, 1967.

Lenneberg, E. H.: On explaining language. *Science, 164(*3880):635, 1969.

Lesser, G., Fifer, G., and Clark, D. H.: *Mental Abilities of Children From Different Social-Class and Cultural Groups.* Monograph of the Society for Research in Child Development, Serial No. 102, 1965.

Lieberman, P., Crelin, E. S., and Klatt, D. H.: Phonetic ability and related anatomy of the newborn and adult human, Neanderthal man, and the chimpanzee. *American Anthropology, 74:*287, 1972.

Lipsitt, L. P.: Learning in the human infant. In Stevenson, H. W., Hess, E. H., and Rheingold, H. L. (Eds.): *Early Behavior.* New York, Wiley, 1967, pp. 225-247.

Lipsitt, L. P.: Infant learning: The blooming, buzzing, confusion revisited. Remarks made at the Second Washington Symposium on Learning, Bellingham, Washington, October 22-23, 1970. Proceedings published in Meyer, M. E. (Ed.): *Second Western Symposium on Learning: Early Learning.* Western Washington State College, 1971.

Loban, W. D.: *The Language of Elementary School Children.* Champaign, National Council of Teachers of English, 1963.

MacNeilage, P. F.: Motor control of serial ordering of speech. *Psychological Review,* 77:182, 1970.

McDonald, L. B.: *The Development and Evaluation of a Program for Prospective Teachers: Decoding and Encoding Black Dialect.* Unpublished doctoral dissertation, Bloomington, Indiana University, 1971.

McNeil, D.: Developmental psycholinguistics. In Smith, F., and Miller, G. A. (Eds.): *The Genesis of Language: A Psycholinguistic Approach.* Cambridge, M.I.T. Press, 1966a.

McNeill, D.: A study of word association. *Journal of Verbal Learning and Verbal Behavior,* 5:548, 1966b.

McNeill, D.: *The Development of Language.* New York, Harper & Row, 1970a.

McNeill, D.: *The Acquisition of Language: The Study of Developmental Psycholinguistics.* New York, Harper & Row, 1970b.

Menyuk, P.: Children's learning and reproduction of grammatical and nongrammatical phonological sequences. *Child Development,* 39(3):849, 1968a.

Menyuk, P.: The role of distinctive features in children's acquisition of phonology. *Journal of Speech and Hearing Research,* 11:138, 1968b.

Menyuk, P.: *Sentences Children Use.* Cambridge, M.I.T. Press, 1969.

Mercer, J. R.: *Labeling the Mentally Retarded.* Berkeley, University of California Press, 1973.

Miller, G. A.: A psychological method to investigate verbal concepts. *Journal of Mathematical Psychology,* 6:161, 1969.

Miller, W., and Ervin, S.: The development of grammar in child language. In Bellugi, U., and Brown, R. (Eds.): *The Acquisition of Language.* Monograph of the Society of Research in Child Development, 29(92): 9, 1964.

Mlodnosky, L. B.: *Some Child-Rearing Antecedents of Readiness for School.* Unpublished doctoral dissertation, Stanford, Stanford University, 1962.

Moore, D.: Language research in preschool language training. In Lavatelli, C. (Ed.): *Language Training in Early Childhood Education.* Champaign, University of Illinois Press, 1971.

Moore, T. E. (Ed.): *Cognitive Development and the Acquisition of Language.* New York, Academic Press, 1973.

Morse, P. A.: Infant speech perception: A preliminary model and review of the literature. In Schiefelbusch, R. L., and Lloyd, L. L. (Eds.): *Language Perspectives: Acquisition, Retardation, and Intervention.* Baltimore, University Park Press, 1974.

Naremore, R. C.: *Teachers' Judgment of Children's Speech: A Factor*

Analytic Study of Attitudes. Unpublished doctoral dissertation, University of Wisconsin, 1969.

Neisser, U.: *Cognitive Psychology.* New York, Appleton-Century-Crofts, 1967.

Nelson, K.: Concept, word, and sentence: Interrelations in acquisition and development. *Psychological Review, 81*(4):267, 1974.

Norman, D. A.: *Memory and Attention.* New York, Wiley, 1969.

Olim, E.: Maternal language styles and the cognitive development of children. In Williams, F. (Ed.): *Language and Poverty: Perspectives on a Theme.* Chicago, Markham, 1970.

Olmsted, D. L.: A theory of the child's phonology. *Language, 42:*531, 1966.

Palermo, D. D., and Molfese, D. L.: Language acquisition from age five onward. *Psychological Bulletin, 78:*409, 1972.

Pavenstedt, E. (Ed.): *The Drifters.* Boston, Little, Brown and Co., 1967.

Piaget, J.: *Judgment and Reasoning in the Child.* New York, Harcourt, Brace, 1928.

Piaget, J.: *Play, Dreams and Imitation in the Child.* New York, Norton, 1951.

Piaget, J.: *The Language and Thought of the Child.* (Translated by Marjorie Gabain.) New York, Meridith, 1955.

Piaget, J.: Piaget's theory. In Mussen, P. H. (Ed.): *Carmichael's Manual of Child Psychology.* New York, Wiley, 1970.

Piaget, J.: *Biology and Knowledge.* Chicago, University of Chicago Press, 1971.

Piaget, J., and Inhelder, B.: *The Psychology of the Child.* New York, Basic Books, 1969.

Perfetti, C. A.: Psychosemantics: Some cognitive aspects of structural meaning. *Psychological Bulletin, 78:*241, 1972.

Pisoni, D.: *On the Nature of Categorical Perception of Special Sounds.* Unpublished doctoral dissertation, University of Michigan, 1971, Reproduced as supplement to Haskins Laboratory Status Report on Speech Research, 1971.

Plant, J. S.: *The Envelope.* New York, The Commonwealth Fund, 1950.

Rau, L., Mlodnosky, L. B., and Anastasiow, N. J.: Child-rearing antecedents of achievement behaviors in second-grade boys. Final Report on USOE Cooperative Research Project No. 1838, Stanford University, 1964.

Riegel, K.: The language acquisition process: A reinterpretation of selected research findings. In Goulet, L. R., and Baltes, P. B. (Eds.): *Theory and Research in Life-Span Developmental Psychology.* New York, Academic Press, 1970.

Scarr-Salapatek, S.: Race, social class, and IQ. *Science, 174:*1285, 1971.

Schaefer, E. S., and Bayley, N.: *Maternal Behavior, Child Behavior, and*

Their Interactions From Infancy Through Adolescence. Monograph of the Society for Research in Child Development, *28*:1, 1963.

Schiefelbusch, R. L., and Lloyd, L. L. (Eds.): *Language Perspectives: Acquisition, Retardation and Intervention.* Baltimore, University Park Press, 1974.

Semmel, M. I.: Language behavior of mentally retarded and culturally disadvantaged children. *Fifth Annual Distinguished Lecture Series in Special Education,* Los Angeles, University of Southern California, 1966.

Sinclair-de Zwart, H.: Developmental psycholinguistics. In Elkind, D., and Flavell, J. H. (Eds.): *Studies in Cognitive Development: Essays in Honor of Jean Piaget.* Oxford, Oxford University Press, 1969.

Sinclair-de Zwart, H.: Language acquisition and cognitive development. In Moore, T. E. (Ed.): *Cognitive Development and the Acquisition of Language.* New York, Academic Press, 1973.

Skinner, B. F.: *Verbal Behavior.* New York, Appleton, 1957.

Slobin, D. I. (Eds.): *A Field Manual for Cross-Cultural Study of the Acquisition of Communicative Competence.* Berkeley, University of California, 1967.

Slobin, D. I.: *Psycholinguistics.* Glenview, Scott, Foresman, 1971.

Slobin, D. I.: Cognitive prerequisites for the development of grammar. In Ferguson, C. A., and Slobin, D. I. (Eds.): *Studies in Child Language Development.* New York, Holt, Rinehart, and Winston, 1973.

Slobin, D. I., and Welsh, C. A.: Elicited imitation as a research tool in developmental psycholinguistics. In Ferguson, C. A., and Slobin, D. I. (Eds.): *Studies in Child Language Development.* New York, Holt, Rinehart and Winston, 1973.

Smith, F.: *Understanding Reading.* New York, Holt, Rinehart and Winston, 1971.

Snow, C. E.: Mothers' speech to children learning language. *Child Development, 43*(2):549, 1972.

Skodak, M., and Skeels, H. M.: A final follow-up study of one hundred adopted children. *Journal of Genetic Psychology, 75*:85, 1949.

Sperry, L. W.: Hemisphere deconnection and unity in conscious awareness. *American Psychologist, 23*(10):723, 1968.

Spitz, R. A.: Anaclitic depression. *Psychoanalytic Study of Children, 2*:313, 1946.

Stedman, D. J., Anastasiow, N. J., Dokecki, P. R., Gordon, I. J., and Parker, R. K.: How can effective early intervention programs be delivered to potentially retarded children? Report No. OS:72-305-DHEW, Department of Health, Education and Welfare, October, 1972.

Templin, M. C.: Certain language skills in children, their development and interrelationships. Minneapolis, University of Minnesota Press, Institute of Child Welfare Monograph Series, No. 26, 54, 1957.

Terman, L. M.: et al.: *Genetic Studies of Genius: Mental and Physical*

Traits of a Thousand Gifted Children. Stanford, Stanford University Press, 1925, vol. I.

Vygotsky, L. S.: *Thought and Language.* Cambridge, M.I.T. Press, 1962.

Weikart, D. P.: *Ypsilanti Carnegie Infant Education Project: Progress Report.* Ypsilanti, Ypsilanti Public School, Department of Research and Development, 1969.

Werner, H., and Kaplan, B.: *Symbol Formation.* New York, Wiley, 1963.

Werner, E. E., Bierman, J. M., and French, F. E.: *The Children of Kauai,* Honolulu, University Press of Hawaii, 1971.

White, R. W.: Motivation reconsidered: The concept of competence. *Psychological Review, 66:*297, 1959.

AUTHOR INDEX

A

Anastasi, A., 4, 151
Anastasiow, N. J., 4, 6, 8, 26, 53, 54, 60, 63, 117, 118, 145, 151, 157, 158
Anderson, S. A., 27, 151
Anglin, J. M., 46, 151
Asher, J., 144, 151

B

Badger, E., 155
Baer, D. W., 56
Bandura, A., 14, 53, 151
Baratz, J. C., 7, 64, 70, 151, 152
Bartlett, F. C., 51, 152
Bayley, N., 15, 157
Bee, H. L., 55, 152
Beh, W., 27, 151
Bellugi, 26, 39, 152, 154
Bereiter, C., 6, 63, 152
Berko, J., 152
Berlyne, D. E., 6, 152
Bernstein, B., 54, 152
Bever, T. G., 25, 152
Bierman, J. M., 159
Bijou, S. W., 56
Birch, H. G., 9, 152
Bovet, M., 155
Bower, G. H., 27, 152
Bowlby, J., 5, 152
Braine, M. D. S., 39, 152
Brown, R., 25, 26, 27, 39, 152, 154
Butterfield, E. C., 35, 63, 152

C

Cairns, G. F., 35, 152
Castaneda, A., 144, 152
Castaneda, C., 12, 153
Caudill, W., 14, 153
Cazden, C. B., 19, 55, 68, 69, 153

Chilman, C. S., 55, 153
Chomsky, N., 19, 20, 153
Clark, D. H., 13, 155
Clark, M., 152
Coles, R., 10, 17, 153
Condon, W. S., 35, 45, 153
Crelin, E. S., 155
Cronbach, L. J., 5, 153

D

Davis, A., 4, 5, 34, 153
Deutsch, C., 153
Deutsch, M., 6, 54, 63, 153
Dewey, 45, 47
Dokecki, P. R., 158

E

Eimas, P. D., 35, 154
Engelmann, S., 6, 63, 152
Entwisle, D. R., 154
Ervin, S., 39, 41, 154, 156

F

Ferguson, C. A., 154
Fifer, G., 13, 155
Flavell, J. H., 23, 24, 27, 49, 154
Fodor, J., 19, 154
Fraser, C., 26, 39, 152, 154
Frasure, N. E., 154
French, F. E., 159
Furth, H. G., 26, 154

G

Garrett, M., 19, 154
Ginsberg, H., 5, 17, 60, 154
Gordon, I. J., 56, 158
Goslin, D. A., 154
Gray, S., 6, 154
Gupta, W., 67
Guskin, J., 58, 154
Gussow, J. D., 9, 69, 152, 154

161

SUBJECT INDEX

A

Accommodation, 48
Appalachian poor, 11
Articulation, 60
Assimilation, 48

B

Berko Test, 61
Bilingualism, 4, 15, 144-145

C

Closure, grammatical, 61
Cognitive orientation, 6, 21, 25
Competence, linguistic, 19
Conventional symbolic system, 22
"Cultural difference phenomenon," 4

D

Deafness, 26
Decoding, 19
Deep structure, 19
DISTAR Language Program, 143
Drill-and-practice curriculum, 6
Durham Educational Improvement Project, 148

E

Economic levels, 9
Emotional development, 11
Encoding, 19

F

Free-recall tasks, 27
Fricatives, 37
Function word omissions, 64, 111-141

G

Genetic constraints, 6, 7
Grammatical closure, 61

H

Hampton Institute Nongraded Follow Through Model, 145
Holophrasic speech, 38
Horizontal structuring, 42

I

Idiosyncratic symbolic system, 22
Illinois Test of Psycholinguistic Abilities (ITPA), 63
Imitation, 21, 53
Intelligence, 5, 145
  birth, at, 13
IQ, 5

J

Japanese Tokugawa ethic, 13

L

Locatives, 26

M

Maternal-separation studies, 5
Mental imaging, 21
Mental retardates, 117
Migrant workers, 10, 11
Mimicking, 21
Mnemonics, 51
Modeling, 142, 143

N

Negative attraction, 70

O

Open class, 39

P

Paradigmatic processing, 28
Peabody Picture Vocabulary Test, 63

165